Phoenix Rising

Phoenix Rising

No-Eyes' Vision of the Changes to Come

Mary Summer Rain

The Donning Company/Publishers
Norfolk/Virginia Beach

Other books by Mary Summer Rain

Spirit Song
Dreamwalker

First Printing   July 1987
Second Printing October 1987
Third Printing   March 1988

The Donning Company/Publishers
5659 Virginia Beach Boulevard
Norfolk, Virginia 23502

Library of Congress Cataloging-in-Publication Data

Rain, Mary Summer.
   Phoenix rising.

   Sequel to: Spirit song.
   1. No-Eyes, 1892?-1984. 2. Chippewa Indians—Biography. 3. Shamans—Colorado—Biography. 4. Chippewa Indians—Religion and mythology. 5. Chippewa Indians—Medicine. 6. Indians of North America—Religion and mythology. 7. Indians of North America—Medicine. 8. Psychical research—Colorado—Biography. I. Title.
   E99.C6N645   1987   978.8'00497   87-6724
   ISBN 0-89865-528-5 (pbk.)

Printed in the United States of America

There are those who are skeptics. There are those who are doubters. And there are those who prefer to don rose-colored glasses. To these ones, I have no words; for they have made their choice, though the signs have been many.

Yet there are those who wonder. There are those who have gentle stirrings. And there are those who have stepped upon the beautiful threshold of awareness—all on the verge of perceiving that which is there to see. To these ones, I say, open your exquisite senses. Look with fine clarity into that which is beyond and beneath, within and without. In these coming critical times, listen to and heed the directives of your spirits that retain the high wisdom you are just now perceiving.

And still, there are those who know. There are those who, within their tender hearts, have seen, felt, and recognized that which is there to see. There are those whose precious heritage has made them the silent preservers of that which is to be. To these ones, I have no words, for they already know the Words—ancient wisdom words that have stood eternal and pure since they were first given, ever triumphantly surviving the vulgar ravages of time.

phoenix (fe niks) n. *Egyptian Mythology* A bird that consumed itself by fire after 500 years, and rose renewed from its ashes. Symbolically represents rebirth, renewal of life and resurrection of Truth. A symbol of eternal life.

...AND THE GREAT PHOENIX WAS SEEN RISING UP FROM THE SMOLDERING ASHES OF THE EARTH. ITS IRIDESCENT PURPLE FEATHERS CATCHING THE SUNLIGHT AND REFLECTING BLINDING BEACONS OUT ONTO THE LAND—BEACONS THAT WERE THE SIGN OF THE WORLD'S REGENERATION, ITS NEW AGE OF AWARENESS AND ETERNAL PEACE.

Contents

Author's Foreword

Many paths appear to be correctly marked. They are cleverly disguised with all the appropriate signs, yet a nebulous silent beckoning leads you in the opposite direction and you follow your inner promptings.

Many roads are smoothly paved. They are bordered with the fresh scent of vibrant dew-flecked flowers. They literally reek of sun-drenched valleys and are filled with the mystical essence of love that attempts to draw you forward. They are but masterful illusions. They are a contrived device to mislead and tempt the unwary and the exhausted soul.

When I reached the towering sentinels of the snowy Rocky Mountains of Colorado, I knew that my physical path had abruptly ended. The rest was left to the powers that be. I had silent promptings to accomplish important spiritually related work. I was psychically sensing such an amazing urgency of time to get going—yet, I knew not what I was supposed to do. The inevitable signs of worldly decomposition were flashing like neon warnings all around me. As time ticked on I could plainly see them escalating, yet I remained locked within the dark void of a confining limbo, never being able to move forward with my unknown spiritual purpose. I became increasingly impatient with the terribly frustrating situation. I knew in my heart, by the way the mystical essence of the mountains permeated through to my being and consumed my spirit, that I was indeed in the correct geographical location, yet I was as a lone schooner with lifeless sails drifting endlessly upon a glassy spiritual sea. I needed some explosive form of impetus to breathe life into my hovering spirit and billow it onward toward the final landing dock of my path's intended destination.

In a moment of heavy desperation, I drove far up into the virgin stillness of the Pike National Forest. I left my old pickup and weaved my way on foot through the rich depths of the thriving viridescent forest. The innocent beauty accepted me as I was. It filled me with a profound comfort that deepened with every step I took. It filled my soul. It overflowed. And I cried.

Great sobs pierced the glistening green silence. I cried from the continued desperation, from years of aloneness, from the sense of urgency and not being able to do anything about it. I cried for the unaware masses, for the confirmed unbelievers and for the world. And I cried for myself.

Suddenly, a familiar psychic sensation crept slowly up my back, and its chilling icy fingernails pricked each hair on my neck. My head crawled. I was no longer alone. My highly prized solitude had been shattered by an unknown invading presence. My mind informed me that nobody could possibly be in this secluded section of the woodlands, yet my keen radar was beeping wildly out of control. Cautiously, I raised my head slightly and peered over my arms. And, standing some distance away, was an old wrinkled woman. How strange. She was merely observing me. With coal black eyes that appeared to stab through to my very soul, she stared unmoving.

I tensed and watched.

The figure remained motionless between the jackpines—listening. The dark pools of her eyes seemed to be glazed with the swirling motion of mercury.

My mind frantically raced through its computer banks. This was a new one for me. Somewhat embarrassed, I wiped my eyes and raised my head to confront the rude intruder.

The old one spoke with an unexpected steady note of authority. She informed me that she lived in a nearby cabin.

I quickly apologized for trespassing onto her private property. I turned to leave.

Then she shouted my name, a name she could not possibly know.

I froze in mid-step as I felt the warming sensation of my spiritual sails begin to billow full with a new refreshing type of wind. My ship docked with a firm thud against the strong impetus my weary soul had been aimlessly drifting toward.

The old one was a Chippewa medicine woman by the name of No-Eyes. She was meant to intersect my path at this precise juncture of time in order to enrich it with a deeper direction—an inner one.

In time, the two of us cemented an unbreakable bond of a unique friendship over the next two years. She, the high spiritual teacher; I, the simple novice trying desperately to absorb her unfailing and unmatched wisdom. We spent our days of instruction within the homey atmosphere of her meager cabin.

The passing seasons had no ill effect on my regular visits. The harsh winter wind would howl like a crazed banshee while it flung great masses of heavy snow against her rattling windows, yet inside, we were warmed by a blazing fire and our unconventional relationship. Springtime sent up giddy greetings of joy from the forest life that was budding forth around us. Summer gave us many happy occasions to take our exacting lessons out into the warm sunshine. And in autumn, we treaded the crisp-fallen aspen leaves and allowed the golden drowsiness of nature to bid us a temporary farewell before its final nod into hibernation.

We talked of ordinary daily life. We shared mystical journeys through time and other newly revealed dimensions. We would take our lesson breaks and become momentarily playful by joining our spirits with that of the mighty graceful falcon in his silent flight through his lush mountain valleys.

We shared this way for two years. And then she returned to her birthland to die.

In those two magnificent years I spent with my friend, No-Eyes, we talked of many wondrous things. She was a mountain of logic. She was a citadel of wisdom. Yet, no subject was more importantly pressing for her to reveal than what she referred to as the rising of The Great Phoenix again. It was a subject that continually demanded my utmost serious and centered attention.

The days of this Phoenix lesson material were exceedingly difficult for me to endure. She was always gravely serious. I didn't like the subject matter because it was so terribly depressing, yet I knew it was vital that I hear her out. I didn't want to listen, but I had to. I had to know the warning signals, the final signs of our world-in-change, the signs of Phoenix rising.

The above was written in 1984. I regret that, for reasons far beyond my control, this timely book has been delayed in reaching the public. Consequently, I feel it's of the utmost importance for the readers of *Phoenix Rising* to be fully mindful that the entire content of this book is a precise rendering of exact conversations that took place in 1982.

I am therefore saddened that several of the old one's visions for the future have already come to pass during the long interim between the writing of this manuscript and its eventual, long-awaited release date. I cannot help that which I had no control over.

When the catastrophic Russian meltdown occurred at Chernobyl, I was devastated to think that perhaps now people would consider this book as being "after the fact." Nevertheless, out of deep respect for my beloved visionary, I have left the original text unaltered—just as it was written back in 1984. And I would therefore, hope and pray that

No-Eyes' impeccable credibility has only been enhanced because of this unfortunate delay in the eventual publication of her timely words of wisdom.

I'm sorry, No-Eyes, you know I did my ultimate best to reach the people in time.

Mary Summer Rain
1987

Contractions

*The Earth rumbled beneath the
surface of the land.
It rumbled with the strained
contractions of the Earth Mother's
new labor.*

I loved my beautiful days with No-Eyes. I loved the old one dearly. Her long grey hair was always neatly tied back with a rawhide string at the nape of her thin neck, trailing a coarse thick braid down to her waist. She wore old calico skirts that reached to mid-calf. Her tattered black stockings showed signs of countless mending. And she shuffled around on beautifully beaded moccasins. She was truly comical to look upon, with the absence of teeth and those huge coal black sightless eyes; yet to me, she was most lovely, for her mystic wisdom shone bright and her boundless compassion was matched only by her deep love of all living things.

The season was autumn. I loved autumn too. It was the time when all of nature screamed out to be noticed before it bowed out of the limelight for a while. The deep intensity of vibrant colors pierced my senses with a saber-sharp clarity. The aspens blanketed the vast deeply sloped mountainsides by pulling up a magnificently embroidered quilt of yellow and vivid orange. And the lowering western sun would magically gilt the serrated edges of each individual leaf at sunset. The clear air was filled with a crisp new freshness that forewarned of woodgathering. And the heady scent of swirling woodsmoke filled my entire being.

I thought of all these delectable characteristics of autumn as I made my leisurely way to my dear friend's cabin. And I was filled with an inner peace that was far beyond the reach of simple description. I was rich. I had reached the end of my long search where I had found a beautiful old woman who readily taught me all she knew. I was rich with the magical facets of the endless beauty of the glorious Rocky Mountain seasons. I was wealthy with the loyal companionship of my husband, Bill, who had faithfully traversed the long and treacherous path by my side. And my three girls were happy and healthy little believers who constantly rejoiced in the innocence of nature. Yes, all these things filled my spirit and gave a permanent meaning to my life. And as I reached the road to my friend's house, I was nearly bursting with love for everything around me. I parked the truck and ran up to the little cabin-on-the-hill that housed my precious teacher. I opened the door.

No-Eyes was clumsily fussing with the fire. She was busily nosing an old iron poker under newly-placed logs.

"Hi, No-Eyes!" I greeted excitedly.

Silence.

I gently closed the door, crossed the small living area and tapped her shoulder.

"I know Summer be here," she barked without bothering to look up.

"What kind of greeting is that?" I teased snapping my hands to my hips.

Her tone softened apologetically. "No-Eyes sorry. I be thinking, that all." Replacing the blackened poker, she pulled up her impaired rocker. "Summer take off blanket now. Sit."

I didn't care for the impressive demand in her voice, however I did as instructed. I couldn't claim to be the perfect student as far as the lessons went, but I did always manage to obey. I removed my heavy woven serape and sat facing her on the old worn couch. "How are you today? Sure is one hell of a gorgeous day out there!" I exclaimed enthusiastically.

"Summer no swear," she testily shot back.

"No-Eyes, that's not really considered swearing, it's just a way of emphasizing a person's words."

A boney finger snaked out to me and rattled vigorously. "No make fancy excuse! That still be swearing."

"Oh all right," I sighed without losing my exuberance. "Still, it doesn't change what I said. Have you been outside yet? It really is beautiful. The early morning sunlight on the aspens is . . . ."

"SUMMER!" She sliced off my sentence with the cold steel blade of her sharp voice.

6

I had begun rambling again about the beauty of autumn. And I figured she was now about to accuse me of being made scatter-brained by the intoxicating effects that autumn had on me.

"Get woodsmoke out of brain! We gonna talk serious today!"

I knew it was too good to be true. She had a curious habit of stealing away my pleasurable autumn musings. And I hated it when she became so deadpan serious. I was either going to make a grave psychic journey or I was going to be subjected to another one of her disheartening world-in-change lectures. I honestly wasn't in the mood for either one. Why couldn't we just go for a little walk in the woods and. . . .

"NO!" She stamped her foot. "Summer gonna hear 'bout new birth on earth. Summer gonna hear 'bout sights and sounds of new signs that be comin'."

My interest was firmly snagged. "What new signs?" I perked.

"Summer not interrupt. Summer gonna hear 'bout Earth Mother in bad labor. She gonna give birth to great something. She already in first labor hours. She be hurting real bad now."

I leaned forward. "What is this great something? What are you talking about?"

Silence.

Then the rocker began to creak and thud the way it did whenever she was excited about something or whenever she was waiting for me to systematically come up with the obvious answers to my own unnecessary questions. I thought to the rhythmic metronome of the rocker. "The changes. You're talking about the final earth changes."

Creak-thud. Creak-thud.

A grave thought floated subliminally through my mind. "No-Eyes, is there more than what we previously saw together?"

Creak-thud. She let her sightless eyes nonchalantly scan the smoke-stained ceiling as she methodically tapped her fingers on her knee.

"There *is* more! You never said there would be more!" I was surprised and hurt all at once. We had discussed the earth changes before and she had never even hinted at anything more coming about.

Her eyes slowly shifted from the ceiling to bore into mine. "Summer never ask," she replied with a calculative smoothness.

"I didn't think I *had* to!"

She shrugged her shoulders and flicked her wrists. "What so, Summer. Before be no good time to tell. Now good time." She made it appear so matter-of-fact. So simple.

It was neither. I didn't want to hear anymore about the negative things that were coming for humanity. I had seen enough coming attractions to have a good enough idea of what the movie would be like. It plagued me with a terribly heavy empathy for the human masses, especially those who refused to listen to the warnings or to believe in the signs. It was such a beautiful day, I just wanted to walk in the woodlands and let its spirit flow into my absorbing senses. I sighed deeply and resigned myself to the heaviness of her coming words. I had no choice in the matter.

"That better. Summer no want to hear. Summer listen anyways." She cocked her head in a questioning attitude. "How Summer gonna know signs if I no tell?"

I was disgusted. "I'll know. And besides, they're already here."

"Blah!" she blurted waving her hands in the air, "that *no* stuff. That only what-so stuff. Summer gonna hear it *all* now. Summer gonna tell people stuff to see, stuff to hear!"

I wasn't enthused about her brainy idea. "No-Eyes," I sighed again, "I hate to rain on your parade, but I told you before that people don't listen, they only hear what they want to hear." This was getting old—very old.

"What so 'bout parade?" she questioned with a frown.

"That's just a figure of speech. What I mean is, I hate to ruin your honorable idea of warning people, but . . . ."

The rocker abruptly tilted forward as she stretched her frail body and craned her neck toward me. "Summer no ruin no stuff here," she threatened softly. "Summer tell stuff, that all. It be simple." The chair creaked erratically. She had spoken.

We were obviously at odds again as we so often were. She kept up the frantic creak and thud.

I tried to smooth over our jagged impasse. "Listen, I'm sorry. So I convey your signs. I do my part, but what if nobody listens or believes? Then what good was it all for? It'll only make me look like some grimy gloom and doomsday sayer in ashes and sackcloth."

Silence.

"Well? Won't I look like that?" I pushed.

Creak-thud. Creak-thud.

That was it. I ran out of patience. "*No-Eyes!* Will you *please* stop that *damned* rocking and *answer* me!"

Silence. Slower rocking.

I sighed and slouched defeatedly down into the lumpy couch. She could be so blasted exasperating at times.

Then a gentle voice whispered through thin lips. "I not gonna talk 'bout stuff if Summer gonna swear," she pouted.

Oh God, she was so touchy. "Okay, I'm sorry I swore, but please, just answer me when I ask you something. No-Eyes," I pleaded, "It's very difficult to carry on a decent conversation with you when you answer me with silence. I'm willing to listen to you but I'm too tired for more of these games."

"What so! No games here. Summer need think stuff out. I not gonna be 'round for answers all times."

"I know that, but couldn't we just get on with it for today?"

Grinning wide, she slapped her knee. "Yep! We gonna get on with stuff now."

Relief. I made myself more comfortable. The couch was old and lumpy from many years use, but I had a particular way of sitting on it that was reasonably lump-free. I squirmed down into it and prepared myself for a very long and depressing day.

The old woman slid her chair closer to the couch and sat quietly for a few minutes. She often did this to get inside my head to check if I was truly prepared to listen well. Then, she reached for my hand.

I leaned forward to hold her boney fingers. I was all ears.

"Summer, I gonna talk 'bout serious stuff here. I not get all stuff talked 'bout in one day. We gonna need many days even. This one big long lesson."

I was finally resigned to the depressing lecture and I told her that I understood. "I know, No-Eyes. I realize that there must be a great deal more that we never covered concerning the final years. You can count on me, I'll listen carefully."

She patted my hand. "Summer need do more than listen. Summer need to remember. Summer need to be able to remember 'nough to tell peoples 'bout all signs here. That most important." She was remaining adamant about me telling people about her foreseen signs.

I forfeited my former argument. "Do you want me to go out to the truck for my notebook?"

"Nope. Summer can remember. We gonna spend one day on one stuff (subject). That way Summer gonna remember easy."

"Go ahead. I'm ready."

Again she patted my hand and squeezed tightly for a moment before resting back into the chair. The gentle rocking motion began. "Summer, Earth Mother be in great pain. She be in great pain now, even as we speak. She get ready to give birth to newborn. This newborn been here many moons before. It coming out again from between Earth Mother's legs. Listen, Summer, listen hard and you hear the quickened heartbeat inside Earth Mother. She now in hard contractions of her greatest labor."

I was puzzled. "I'm not sure I follow. What newborn is coming?"

The old one stealthily bent forward and secretly whispered, "It been here before. It come again, again and again. It not can be destroyed. Think, Summer, think!" She resumed her rocking. She was done talking for now. She had given several clues and left me to my own devices to reach the correct conclusion.

I thought about a thing that couldn't be destroyed. I thought about something that kept coming back again and again. I wondered if she meant God. Then I realized that that idea was most definitely way off base because she was speaking about something that was being born and coming *before* the final battle, something that was to precede the massive changes, or perhaps something whose birth or presence was to effect or herald in the changes. It was certainly too late in time for another world leader-type to be born. Besides, a physical leader could be destroyed. It was too late in time for her to mean the physical birth of anyone. Therefore, she must be referring to a mystical, symbolic birth. That singular thought brought to mind all of the classic characters in Greek mythology and yet, as I reviewed them, they didn't actually match up either. Then the obvious answer speared my mind like a bolt of blue lightning.

The old lady literally beamed with affirmation. She had evidently been meticulously following my systematic mental eliminations, because when I thought of it, she confirmed it with her wide toothless grin. She slapped her knee.

I sheepishly grinned back. Then became serious again. "The Phoenix. Right?"

"That take long time. That okay. Summer get right answer anyways. Yup, it be great Phoenix that gonna rise up again just like all times ago. He already there." She pointed to the floor, meaning under the earth. "He been forming for years now. He all ready to break out of Earth Mother's womb. If peoples quiet themselves, they gonna feel the labor contractions of Earth Mother. She be so, so tired. She gonna give up great Phoenix soon. Summer see."

I thought long on her words. Things were still too undefined for me yet. What were these birth pangs she spoke of? Surely she didn't mean the earth changes, for it was a little too early for those. She had to mean a more indirect type of new movement. I speculated more on it while she cleverly waited for me to sort it out.

I always combed the daily newspapers for new evidence of the changing times. What stood out most prominently in my mind was the seemingly sporadic, yet steady, decline of our nation's business and economy. I snuck a furtive glance at the calm old woman. She was attempting to cloak her smile.

I had been right. "So the labor contractions of the Phoenix have a direct bearing on the condition of the general economy."

"It have to do with *all* money stuff. That economy? What so! Phoenix be making great movements under Earth Mother. Monies, all business stuff gonna suffer here."

"No-Eyes, does the Phoenix create the ills of the economy?"

She was visibly outraged by my erroneous supposition. "Blah! Phoenix not *create* no bad stuff. He gonna come to rise again to bring in new times to peoples, new age, new stuff."

"Then why are you appearing to interconnect the two in respect to the negative aspects?"

"'Cause they *are* connected, that why!" She was through with her end of my present line of inquiry.

I figured it was my turn to sort out the rest. If it was true that the ills of the general economy were indeed connected with the birthing of the new Phoenix, and yet the Phoenix didn't actively effect those ills, then the two were independent of each other. No, that wasn't quite right either. I thought harder, deeper. She had said that the Phoenix was rising again to herald in a new age. And that that age would be a renewed world of mankind. That was it! It was time for the world to experience the *beginnings* of change. And the Phoenix had also reached its time to coincide its *freedom* with the *end* of the changes. That made absolute sense to me. The changes were now beginning to become evident just as the birth of the Phoenix was. And when the changes were complete, so would the Phoenix be.

No-Eyes leaned forward to jab at my knee. "Summer think pretty okay today," came the gleeful cackle.

I chuckled at her unique way with words. "Well, it all makes logical sense really. I guess when you think about it, mankind is the one who is creating all the changes. And the new-rising Phoenix will be there to bring about the peace and rejuvenation to what is left of that purged mankind."

She nodded in time with the gentle rocking motion of her chair. "Now we gonna talk 'bout all bad monies stuff coming on top of Earth Mother while Phoenix be moving 'round under Earth Mother, in her belly."

"If I may interrupt, does this mean the prophesied trouble within the stock market?"

The sparkle of her mind was suddenly dulled with a murky scrim of puzzlement that shaded her eyes.

I explained the new term.

She appeared unconcerned. "What so! That only be tiny corner of stuff here. Summer listen now. I not know all right names for words here, but I gonna need a tiny help so Summer can get stuff right."

I smiled with understanding. "All right, I'll try to fit in the correct words to your meanings. Go slow so I'm sure I understand what you're saying." Then something struck me as being rather incongruous and I couldn't help but to inquire about it. "No-Eyes, I've never doubted your wise words, but how can you know of things to come when you are not aware of the exact terminology and the everyday technicalities of the modern world? Do you see what I'm getting at?"

She bristled with indignation. "Humph! Summer think No-Eyes be dumb 'cause I not know right words!"

Her reply was pure paranoia. It irritated me. "You *know* that's not what I meant! That wasn't even fair!"

"What so! What fair, Summer? Listen, babies see bottles. They know what that be. They know they want that. Do tiny baby *say* 'bottle'? Summer drive old truck. Summer know how insides work? Summer know all right names for all inside stuff? Huh, Summer? Huh?"

"No," I admitted honestly wishing I'd never brought up the subject.

"I not always know right *names* for stuff, but I still know 'bout stuff. See?"

"All right, I see," I sighed. "I'm sorry I upset you. Yet you really shouldn't take my off-handed questions to heart the way you do."

Thin shoulders lifted and dropped. "Maybe so. Maybe no. We go into monies stuff now."

"Good!" I snapped a bit too hastily.

She frowned. "Summer got smart mouth now?"

"Oh dammit, No-Eyes! Would you just get on with it!"

She flashed me a contrived look of pain. "Summer no swear at No-Eyes," came the soft request while she dropped her head to study her faded skirt.

The pretense hadn't fooled me. I grinned and playfully peered at her through the corner of my eye.

She peeked up through sparse lashes and released a chuckling wheeze of laughter.

We were once again on equal footing. And raising her head proudly, the lesson continued in a lowered tone of renewed serious-ness. "Summer, many peoples have great unrest deep in hearts 'bout who they working for. Many work places not be fair. These working peoples give boss all they got to give. They give and give. They no get stuff back. They gonna stop work. They gonna work again when they get stuff back. Many working peoples all over gonna stop work. They plenty angry. It gonna go on all over."

"It sounds to me like you're talking about strikes—a lot of strikes. No-Eyes," I explained, "a strike is when the workers don't get what's justifiably due them or maybe they don't get good healthy working conditions, so they band together in a unified group. They stop working in order to rightfully obtain those things."

"That what I just say!" she exclaimed adamantly.

I smiled. "Just wanted to clarify it, that's all."

A knobby finger rose in caution. "There be more to this here, Summer. Bosses say workers want too many stuff. Bosses say they no can do business and keep workers happy. Summer know what many, many bosses gonna do?"

I merely shook my head.

"Bosses gonna take business place to other lands. Bosses get good business *and* get good workers all at same time, see? Many peoples here no have job, no have no monies no more." She hesitated before continuing. "They also gonna get machines to do work of workers."

I thought on this last one while she was speaking. I got the clear drift. "These lands you're talking about, are they far away?"

"Yup. They be far over great waters."

And thoughtlessly forgetting about her need for verbal simplification, I excitedly slipped into my own natural vernacular.

"Then you foresee the major companies relocating their factories from America and constructing them overseas where they can operate in a more advantageously cost-effective manner. And they'll also retrofit their remaining American factories to accommodate a greater utilization of computer automation resulting in massive layoffs."

Whispy brows furrowed. "Summer go too fast. What all those words?" She paused a moment and shifted her eyes while mentally checking through her psychic dictionary. "Never mind. Summer be right here," she confirmed. "Summer get that stuff right."

"So, No-Eyes, if a lot of the factories will relocate overseas, won't that also affect our import/export balance?"

"What *that*?" she spouted in agitation.

"The buying and selling of goods between countries."

"Yup. That gonna change too. That gonna get real bad, maybe almost stop even. When that almost stop, many more big business and factories gonna stop too. Many peoples now out of work. No place to work. Many peoples be plenty angry."

"That's bad news. Our government is trimming programs that take care of the poor people now. How are we ever going to care for the thousands more that will be out of work in the future?"

"President do that," she proclaimed confidently as the trusty rocker began to speak again.

I shook my head. "Wrong, No-Eyes. They spend lots of money on new weapons. They siphon off the money from the care programs and pour it all into more and bigger weapons, anti-weapons and defense programs."

She firmly stuck to her six-guns. "No-Eyes just say President gonna do that for poor. Summer got stuff stuck in ears?"

"But I just explained...."

"Summer no explain no stuff! No-Eyes explain here. President have more monies for more poor by making all peoples pay more monies to country, see? It simple."

It was simple all right. "You mean higher taxes. Now I can really see where this is going to lead everything."

"Summer see?" she squeaked. "Summer tell No-Eyes where this stuff gonna lead."

"To one hell of a revolt," I uttered disgustedly.

"Yup. But that stuff gonna be talked 'bout another day with other stuff."

"Oh great, I can barely wait," I whispered under my breath.

Round eyes squinted into dark slits. "Summer got smart mouth again."

"Yeah," I readily admitted, "I think I'm going to need it to keep my sanity here."

"Nope," she perked, "it all gonna work out. Summer see."

"I wish I could be so confident."

She sparked with a sudden jolt of electrified energy. "Summer want to go see?" she pulsed.

I shot up a barrier with my palms. "No! I believe you. I'll just wait for the real thing."

She slumped in a disappointment that clearly indicated that my decision was my loss. "We gonna go on now then. After big business go away from peoples, the tiny ones gonna stop. Many peoples think they be okay, they safe 'cause they have own business, 'cause they no have to work for boss—they all wrong."

"So...you see the small businesses failing too. God, what'd you have to say that for? Small business is the spine of this nation's economy. Now you've really done it."

"I done no thing! Summer still not see stuff right. All peoples still gonna need many small business. The needed kind gonna do okay. No-Eyes mean kind of business people not really need."

Relief. "Well, why will the others fail then?"

"Many money places gonna be no good."

"Money places?"

"Yup. Places where Summer and Bill keep money."

"Banks?"

"What so. Summer better off with money under bed!"

"I get it. If the banks fail, then naturally the businesses can't get their initial start-up loans and improvement or expansion loans."

"That what I just say!" she blurted. "Summer no have to repeat like echo!"

I ignored her outburst. This negative aspect of the economy was showing an escalation of possibly having devastating effects. "If the banks fail, if big businesses take their operations overseas and automate their remaining ones, and industry is plagued with strikes and shutdowns, what does that do to the stock market?"

"What that?"

Again I attempted to explain as best I could in terms she could readily identify with. It wasn't easy.

She slapped her knee and giggled in childlike delight. "That gonna fall like big tree in forest. That gonna be all gone."

"What?" I bellowed.

She jumped at my sudden unexpected reaction. "What so!" she defended. "Summer no have stock anyways."

"No-Eyes, that doesn't matter. A great many people do."

Dark eyes twinkled with ominous mischief. "Not anymore," came the impish singsong reply.

I couldn't understand her uncharacteristic apathy. "People will go crazy if the stock market crashes!"

She calmly brushed off the subject with a disinterested wave of her hand. "We gonna talk 'bout that crazy stuff some other day."

"Terrific. Well what else would possibly go wrong with the economy? You've just about covered everything."

"Nope. Money places gonna stop. They not gonna give out more big monies to build. No more peoples gonna have monies for houses. No more places left to sell houses even."

"What are you saying? Are you calmly sitting there telling me that new construction will stop? That houses will no longer be built? That real estate agents will be a thing of the past? Are you telling me these things, No-Eyes?"

She appeared reticent to answer me. She began her frantic rocking and casually looked around the room.

"No-Eyes?"

Silence. Rocking. Eyes averted up.

I eyed her with the coldness of frozen gunmetal. "No-Eyes, I asked you a question. Are you going to answer me or not?"

"Yup."

Yup *what?*" I demanded impatiently.

"Yup, No-Eyes answer. Yup, that what No-Eyes telling Summer."

Silence.

Creak-thud.

This economy business was going to be a lot worse and farther reaching than I had initially anticipated. It was certainly going to affect all aspects of our monetary system.

The old woman didn't like having to tell me all she saw coming into my bleak future. She was always straightforward and never intentionally held anything back. She just told things straight out, just as she saw them to be.

I sensed she had a few more ugly tidbits up her innocent looking calico sleeve and I urged her to finish it. "It's okay. I realize I need to know these things. Is there anything else you want to tell me?" I had secretly hoped there wasn't.

She hesitated. The rhythmic creak and thud silenced.

I was wrong. "Well you might as well get it out and over with."

"Summer," she began softly, "price of land and houses gonna go way down—it gonna go way down like water through old broken beaver dam."

I nearly jumped out of my skin. "Now *that's* good news! Now you're talking my kind of talk!"

"Nope," she deflated, sticking a verbal pin in my rising balloon. "Many people gonna try to sell house and land to get more monies—to live. They not gonna get 'nough even. They gonna still owe plenty monies. Stuff gonna be like big whirlpool circle going down and down, deep and deeper. It gonna suck way down. It not gonna go up—ever."

After hearing the ramifications, I could see that her serious attitude had justification. "I see what you mean. People pay a lot for their big homes and when the value dramatically plunges, they can't get enough to even cover their existing mortgage payoff."

"What this mortgage stuff, Summer?"

"That's the initial borrowed money people need to pay back to the bank for the cost of their house or land—initial amount plus added interest."

No-Eyes sadly moved her head from side to side. "Peoples want too much monies from bank. They never gonna have way to pay back."

A lengthy pause passed thickly between us before I urged her to wrap up the subject. "Is there anything else you want to tell me while we're on this subject? We might as well have it all said and done with."

"Only tiny stuff," she admitted with a flash of a flicked wrist.

"Like what tiny stuff?"

"Big peoples in big business gonna take many monies. They gonna do stuff like that all over. That all."

She was talking about an escalation in corporate white-collar

16

crime. And I could clearly understand the reasons for the strong temptations. I looked into the old woman's sad face and tried to comfort her. "No-Eyes, I suppose these things you've told me today are inevitable. I don't want you to feel responsible for them just because you foresaw them becoming a reality. People will survive these economic hardships. People have always managed to endure through the ages. And this will be no different." I smiled warmly. "We're a hardy breed. We'll all manage." I moved from the couch to sit on the floor beside her chair. Her frail hands were cold.

"Summer, I not be sad for me. No-Eyes feel sad for stuff Summer gonna live through." A faraway look glassed her eyes. "I no have to see bad stuff."

"Then I'm happy for you." And I wrapped my arms around her small waist.

"Summer?"

"Yeah?"

"Hear that?"

I listened. I quieted my breathing. And I listened to the nearly inaudible moans of the Earth Mother's strained labor.

The old one softly whispered. "Summer, you come again tomorrow. We gonna talk 'bout what stuff gonna happen when Phoenix coming out of Earth Mother."

I hugged her tenderly. "All right, No-Eyes. I'll be here." I stoked the fire and we spent the remainder of the afternoon sharing in the silent companionship of our warm friendship.

Emerging

*And the crowning of the newborn
Phoenix rent the loins of the
suffering Earth Mother.*

It was Sunday. While I drove through the twisting mountain roads that led to No-Eyes' cabin, I mentally reviewed all that had passed between us the preceding day. I was still somewhat amazed at the intensity of our conversation and at the wide scope which the economic downfall was going to encompass. Literally, no aspect of our present-day monetary system was going to be allowed to escape from some form of negative change.

I previously had known about the fall of the stock market and the insolvency of several of the major banks. Perhaps if I had taken the time to peer behind the writing-on-the wall, I would've foreseen the other obvious changes that would naturally result. It was the domino theory aptly applied to the economic system. It was inevitable.

Bill and I constantly kept a close eye on the newspapers for the upcropping of any of the signs that No-Eyes had foretold. We could see how certain corporate decisions were headed for the final pages of history. More and more indications served to reinforce the beat of our economic dirge. Presently the tune is barely audible. In time, it will gather strength and momentum to reach its climactic crescendo.

We wondered at the dubious future of the industrial strikers. What of all the families of those unfortunate men who labored all their lives for the big companies that will make the decision to relocate their

19

massive plants in other countries or become automated? It seemed to us that money had indeed become the revered golden calf of the nation. Where were the businesses that took care of their workers? Where were the businesses that placed the masses of humanity above their profit margins? Where had human compassion gone?

All these thoughts rudely invaded my woodland drive. Ordinarily this trip would find me extracting gluttonous pleasure from the autumn beauty of the mountains. Not today. Today my heart was heavy with empathy for those who would suffer such great losses in the future. Today I had no time to spoil myself amid the glorious qualities of my precious forest. And it was just as well, for today No-Eyes was going to talk about more changes for my future way of life. I had no indication as to what the subject was going to be, but because of the heaviness I retained from yesterday's discussion, I was mentally and emotionally primed for the negative information I was going to receive.

The turn-off for the cabin was just ahead. The clouds drifted under the sun and all the woods became eerily shrouded. I made the turn and parked the truck. I could see the cabin from where I was and it too was consumed in the spectral greyness. A stranger would've most likely avoided the dilapidated place. In its present shadowed lighting, it appeared desolate and foreboding—a perfect haunting place. However, I was no stranger here. I loved the old place even when it was drenched in the darkness of spellbinding shadows.

I walked the distance up her hill and as I reached her weather-worn steps, the sun burst forth, freeing itself from its temporary murky confines. The bright rays quickly scampered into the wide cracks of the crumbling log chinking and illuminated the old place like a postcard of the Taj Mahal, giving it a warm coating of joy. The sun gave me the high sign, as much to say that even though my teacher had depressing lessons, life was still bright and indeed well worth the trouble of living it. I smiled and entered.

No-Eyes was sitting at her hand-hewn table in the tiny kitchen. Her muted toothless munching always gave me an inner chuckle. I loved the lady so very much.

"What so funny?" she asked through a mouthful of soft grain meal.

"Did I say something was funny?"

"Summer no need speak. No-Eyes hear anyways."

"Can't a person smile around here? Or must I always be as deadpan as you?"

Munch. Munch.

I pulled the heavy serape over my head, laid it on the couch and joined her at the table. "Mind if I join you?"

Without a murmur, she pointed to the wall cupboards and

motioned for me to get my own bowl of natural breakfast. I sat down across from her. "No thanks. I already ate."

"What Summer eat?" she cleverly baited.

"Eggs and grain cakes."

"Summer eat white stuff on eggs?"

"Of course not, those are acid! Hey, you wouldn't be trying to trip me up would you?" I grinned inclining my head toward her as if testing the air.

She shrugged and never answered.

"I know what to eat and what to leave for others," I added.

"Humph!"

I put my chin down near the table and peered up into her eyes. "I love you."

She glanced down at me. The unseeing eyes were misted over.

Reaching for her hand, I held it gently. "I'm fine. I don't mind about today. I know you have to tell me. Let's not make it any harder than it already is." I rubbed the thin skin on her hand. "You better not finish your cereal feeling the way you do." I set the spoon into the wooden bowl and led her into the living room. After pulling up the rocker, I sat her down and knelt beside her. "No-Eyes, I'm so sorry I didn't notice your mood when I came in. There's no excuse for that kind of insensitivity. I should've realized how weighted your spirit must be. Maybe we could save this talk for another time."

She straightened her back and rocked. And that was my only declarative reply. I fluffed up one of the lumpy couch cushions and prepared for my next lesson on the Phoenix chronicles.

For several minutes, silence enveloped the room like an insulating cocoon. I knew she was gathering her thoughts and pulling unto herself a certain measure of peace. Most of my more serious lessons began in this customary manner. I also took the added time to increase my mental awareness and to concentrate on strengthening my memory. I would have to remember all she said, for I used a notebook only twice in the two years worth of lessons. The silence between us became heavier, a sign that we were both well prepared.

"Summer, last time we talk 'bout how Earth Mother start her hard labor with the Phoenix. This time we gonna talk 'bout what happen on earth when great Phoenix show head, when great Phoenix coming out of Earth Mother. Her skin gonna tear bad. Great tears. Her breath be coming in long winds. Her mouth be dry. She be hot then shiver with icy cold. She cry out great amount of tears. She flood stuff with tears."

I realized that the land was as precious to No-Eyes as it was to me. This was the reason for her sadness when I had entered the cabin. She now had to describe the changes on the Earth Mother that were going to affect everyone's life. It grieved her to know these things. It grieved her to have to talk about the pains of the Earth Mother, the mother that so graciously yielded up all her rich bounties to humanity. And now she was going to be split apart and forever scarred.

A lone tear fell from the old one's creviced cheek. She let it fall unnoticed, perhaps she didn't care. What was one tear compared to the millions that were going to be shed by the tribulations of the masses during the coming days?

I remained respectfully silent. To acknowledge her deep sorrow by offering sympathy was not in keeping with our proud heritage. She knew in her heart that I was alongside her in her grief. Many times no words were spoken between us. They were unnecessary. I momentarily joined her spirit and she appeared to be thankful. "That feel good."

I smiled.

"I gonna get no stuff done. No-Eyes better straighten up."

"You don't have to excuse yourself like that. I understand."

"I get on now." There was a short pause before she continued. "Summer, remember I say Phoenix not cause changes? I say all change stuff come at same time Phoenix rising out of Earth Mother?"

"I remember."

"That important here. No can blame Phoenix. He gonna bring new times after change stuff all done," she reiterated.

"Yes, I understand that, No-Eyes."

Inhaling a deep breath, the old one held it a minute and then exhaled slowly. "Summer, peoples already know 'bout big tearing in California. That gonna be most bad one. That one be most bad tear."

"You mean the earthquake."

She nodded. "Summer, many places no have tears happen. Many places no have earth rumble, ever. That gonna change. Big noises gonna come from Earth Mother—deep down inside. They gonna be coming many more times in new places, places where no tears ever be before."

"No-Eyes, those quakes are already showing up. When we lived in the log cabin in Rainbow Valley, we heard the rumble, then we felt the ripple go through the house. It was very eerie. I guess we were more amazed than scared because it was over before we realized what we had experienced. No-Eyes, quakes were extremely uncommon in that area, but recently we've noticed how they have been increasing."

She nodded in semi-agreement before her bottom lip peeled under and she shook her head. "That no big stuff. No-Eyes talk 'bout more and more even. They gonna show up in many new land places.

They gonna get bigger and bigger as Phoenix rise from birthing place. Earth Mother move much under skin. She gonna make big moves."

I thought about his one effect. Surely if the earth was going to be that restless, there was going to be greater consequences. The earth couldn't move that much without having to release the tremendously intensified buildup of pressure. This line of thought naturally led me directly into the subject of volcanoes. It would stand to reason that, logically, if the plates were in such a forceful movement, then the pressure would indeed be unbearable for the earth's delicate crust to retain without more avenues of release.

"No-Eyes, there will be more volcano activity, right?"

She nodded. "Yup. Many more stuff gonna be coming out. This time many more peoples move away. Hot rocks gonna take many houses. Hot rocks be all over stuff. Earth Mother blow and blow stuff all over."

"Now are you talking about Hawaii and Washington State?"

"No-Eyes talk 'bout all over," she defined by extending both arms.

"But there aren't volcanoes all over."

"*Gonna* be!"

"Then you're saying that the dormant volcanoes are going to be hot again."

"No-Eyes say old holes be hot again."

"I guess you mean old craters."

"What that?"

I explained what craters were. I told her about areas where old craters were grown over with trees and that towns were now built on them. I told her about the gold that had been successfully mined from Cripple Creek because of the volcano crater it sits on.

"Tsk-tsk. Town's gonna blow. Peoples better go in big hurry! Summer, I talk 'bout more stuff even. I see land blow high where no land blow before."

"New volcanoes?"

A bobbing head was my answer.

"Well...what about the Rocky Mountains? What about Pikes Peak then?"

She shook her head sadly.

I threw my hands up. "Oh great! Now you're telling me that Pikes Peak is going to blow sky high! No-Eyes, do you know where I live? Woodland Park is the most beautiful little mountain town I've ever seen. It sits right on the Pass..."

"Yup. Summer better move too." She paused. "Maybe Pikes Peak only gonna shudder, rumble some. Summer better move anyway."

This was incredible. "I guess so!"

"There be more stuff."

"Save me the details," I groaned.

"Nope. We gonna finish this."

I rolled my eyes. "Was afraid you'd say that."

She sighed. "Summer, Earth Mother gonna breathe real hard. Phoenix be hard on her. She gonna blow her breath all over. It be fire hot. It gonna dry land up. Big part of land gonna be all dry. It gonna be burned crispy." She paused to allow me to digest that.

And I realized she meant the return of the dust bowl. That was indeed going to have a devastating effect on the food production in America. That was going to herald in all types of food shortages. The dryness was also going to ignite massive widespread fires. This mess was getting messier all the time.

She began again when she saw that I had drawn the necessary conclusions. "That not all Earth Mother's breath gonna do. She gonna blow hard over land. She gonna blow down over farms, through cities, in mountains even. She even blow waters 'round lands. Breath gonna take plenty waters over many lands." Another pause so I could think.

I heard her say only a few sentences, but what she actually said was much. If the wind was going to blow down on farms, cities and mountains alike, then she had to mean tornadoes. Tornadoes were going to increase and be a common occurrence. Also, she mentioned wind from water to land—hurricanes. These are nothing new but, in conjunction with the gravity of the discussion, she meant that their occasion would increase and that their intensity would be more fierce than usual. And when the winds take the waters over the lands, there will be widespread areas of massive flooding. I thought that she had adequately covered the subject of natural disasters when she suddenly began to speak again.

"Earth Mother gonna go like this." She made short panting breaths. "She go like that and make fast, powerful breaths. Many people gonna feel stuff. They gonna die when she do that."

This was confusing to interpret. "By breaths, you mean the wind."

Nod.

"The wind will come up in quick gusts."

Again, another nod. "Fast and hard, like this!" She flashed her arm through the air. "It blow people's cars. It blow people's boats and trains before they know it coming even!"

"Freak accidents will be caused by the sudden strong gusts of wind."

"That so."

"Well, what else?" I sighed.

Her old rocker began its feverish meter. The creak and thud of the uneven legs could be comforting at times, but not this time. She was rocking, not because she was resting, but because she had more to tell. "Many lands fall away, Summer."

"What do you mean? Are you talking about the coastal regions?"

"Nope."

"Inland areas?"

"Nope."

"Islands then."

"Nope."

Getting nowhere fast. "What's left?"

"*Every* land left. Land *all* over gonna be dry, Summer. What dry soil do, huh?"

"It blows away. It doesn't support any worthwhile root system to bind it in place. Erosion! You mean soil erosion from the dry winds! And that will happen all over?"

"Not *all* over," she corrected. "It be 'nough to be big problem. This go with water under Earth Mother drying. Land fall into many big holes all over. When water under earth go dry, earth fall into place where water been."

"Those are called sinkholes, No-Eyes."

"I no care what word Summer use. I tell what I see, that all."

"I know. I just wanted to tell you what that was called."

"I no care," came the stubborn reply.

Sigh.

Creak-thud. Creak-thud.

"No-Eyes, I'm not correcting you, you know."

Silence.

"Are you upset with me?"

Creak-thud. Creak-thud.

I hadn't meant to upset the old one. She was so terribly sensitive. There were too many times that her tender feelings had been easily bruised by a comment I had made. Many times she took unwarranted offense at the modern way I spoke. She didn't understand many of the common phrases and she continually took them to heart.

Suddenly the silence of her rocker brought me out of my private thoughts. I looked at her.

No-Eyes bent forward and whispered through a sly grin. "I not upset. No-Eyes love Summer."

I let out a relieved breath. "I love you too, No-Eyes."

"No-Eyes know. No-Eyes feel that stuff here." She pounded her chest. "And here." She pointed to her forehead.

We shared warm smiles.

"We gonna get on with last stuff now."

"Okay."

"Times in winter be bad. Great storms come. They cover all towns. They gonna be all over. Times in summer gonna be many bad rains too. Much lightning make many fires. Big ice stones gonna come more. They gonna come many more days. Summer and winter be all mix up. It happen all in hour of time."

"Wait a minute. Let me get this straight. The winters will be bad with blizzards and excessive snowfall."

"Yup."

"And the summers will be bad with thunderstorms and large hail."

"Ice stones," she corrected, not wanting to use my word for it.

"Ice stones. Also, the lightning will be worse and do more damage."

Nod. Nod.

"But I don't see how summer and winter gets mixed up in an hour's time?"

"It change hot to cold, see Summer?"

"You mean a rapid drop in temperature?"

"It go up too."

This time I did the nodding.

"That all," she stated definitively.

"That's it?"

She thought a second. "One last stuff. New kind of light in air. Can be in winter. Can be in summer. It like *green*. It be in all air, see?"

I had to honestly admit that I didn't quite see. And she tried once more. "New light in sky. It be green all over. It be in all air all over. See?"

"Do you mean a different coloring will be seen in the sky?"

"Yup. Stuff like that all over in air."

"In the atmosphere."

"That what I already say!" she croaked in exasperation.

"Okay...there will be days that the entire atmosphere, air, is tinged with a greenish hue."

"That right. That what No-Eyes say."

"What is this going to be from?"

Wide eyes become wider. "Summer not know that?"

"Well, let me put it this way. What is it called?"

She was clearly enjoying my loss for proper terms with this one. "Summer not know right word either?"

"Very funny," I gushed sarcastically.

She grinned wide, showing healthy pink gums. "That called *Phoenix Days!*"

26

"Why?" I persisted.

"That be when all stuff coming. That be when all land stuff going on. That when Phoenix coming into world. That be the birthing days of great Phoenix."

"But this greenish hue has got to have a physical source, doesn't it?"

"*Think*, Summer!" she snapped disgustedly.

And I did. I realized that some psychic manifestations *needed* no physical causes. I was duly humbled. "That was a dumb statement I made, huh."

She arched both brows. "Yup. That be dumb all right."

With the cumbersome burden of the earth changes lifted from the frail shoulders of my old friend, she was again able to become light-hearted and more like her old cantankerous self. However, I certainly couldn't say the same for myself, although I dearly wished I could. It would appear that my clever friend had sneakily passed the heavy yoke from her own shoulders onto mine.

I left her cabin that Sunday afternoon with an inner uneasiness that I hadn't experienced for a long while. Being with No-Eyes had made me somewhat complacent, now the old nagging sense of time urgency returned like a psychic slap in the face. I had lost the secure babe-in-arms feeling that her company had given my tired spirit. I was once again rudely shoved out into the cold snow of the bitter reality of the world.

She was a paragon of a teacher and, like a beaver purposefully attacking the delicate bark of an aspen, she had skillfully stripped away my comforting veneer that had served to shield my sensitivity. Once again, my spirit was exposed to the harshness of things-to-come. Once again, my mind was filled with the old troublesome concerns. Once again, my psyche ached with empathy.

Suddenly my mind emptied like water in a holey bucket. It had experienced the dreaded inevitable—a meltdown from all of the depressing devastation that I had heard about in the last two days.

I drove away from the old woman's property, and I had gone nearly three miles before the mental silence engulfed me.

The late afternoon shadows of autumn etched an intricate filigree of lace which undulated across my windshield. I began to take notice of the golden leaves that danced before me across the road in such a carefree manner. A gentle breeze tenderly tugged on the fingertips of the quaking aspens. Smokey rays of sunlight filtered down through the stately jackpines that densely lined the narrow roadway. It was too tempting for me to ignore—I was sinfully weak when it came to the nature of the mountains. I gave in completely as I turned off onto an old overgrown sideroad and drove in for over a mile. I pulled over and got out.

Immediately the wind whispered into my ear. It hinted at mystical woodland days. It foretold of its survival in spite of the terrible changes. It caressed my cheek and tenderly lifted my long hair. I loved it when the wind made attempts at love. It was so sympathetic and caring. Of all the beautiful aspects of the mountains, I loved the wind most of all.

I walked through the pines into a clearing while my etheric companion followed alongside. Somewhere close by, a stream giggled. My friend, the wind, carried the water's wanton laughter to me and I moved toward the gaiety. It was so peaceful, I didn't ever want to leave. The twisting watercourse was narrow, yet the rock and boulder-strewn bottom gave it cause for its constant voice. The soft banks were thoughtfully padded with a thick velvety moss, making a comfortable bed for this weary body.

I removed my moccasins, pulled up the legs of my jeans and sat on the steam's welcome mat. The rushing waters were biting and refreshing all at the same time. I let out an exhausted sigh and looked around at the innocent beauty that surrounded my secret meditation room. I was not alone here. I was in reverent company. I layed back onto the moss and watched the sun make crocheted designs on all she touched. The tall ponderosas murmured age-old secrets to each other. They were no strangers to the esoteric truths of life. The happy stream giggled as it tickled over my legs. And I lost myself to their inebriating essences.

When I again entered into conscious awareness, the sun had journeyed far over the western ridge. The wind made hushing sounds through the pines and the stream excitedly gossiped with the moon about the tales of her mystical journeys. The full moon smiled down at me through his wavering frame of tree tops.

I pulled my numb legs out of the water, still remaining in my restful repose on the bank. I watched the minute movements of the silver moonbeams that reached down through the evergreens. Nature was a world unto its own. Nature, with its vast civilizations of crawling people, winged, finned and four-legged people was a separate world. Nature, with its long-guarded secrets to the mysteries of the universe was where I belonged. Indeed, nature was a most individualized yet compatible reality. And to journey into that unique reality was one of the most beautiful experiences a person could ever hope to achieve. This little piece of forest was at a stage of ultimate peace. It was an antideluvian world that was rich with an innocently radiant beauty. If you attuned your inner sense of hearing, you could hear the precise language of it. You could comprehend the finite vibrations of each of its species of people. You could hear the fascinating history of the century-old tree, see what the stream has seen and know the answers to all the mystifying enigmas of the ages. The forest is ever a faithful friend, but only to those who would believe in it, only to those who joined its spirit. I believed. I joined. I always had.

The moon man winked before he nosed behind the spiney pinnacles of pine, and I was suddenly plunged into a darker night. I could still see well enough, yet I closed my eyes and listened intently. I heard a lone coyote yip and howl for its lost mate. The trees hushed as the wind rocked them to sleep. Several owls hooted to one another. In the thick willows beside me, a small creature stirred. To my right, a squatting porcupine made its waddling way into its cozy home in a hollow log. Here and there a bird chirped its goodnight salutation to anyone that would listen. The crisp-fallen leaves crunched under the scurrying paws of a late night kaibab squirrel. The night mountain forest was alive and thriving. It assured me of the fact that life would continue to endure no matter how many changes came about on the land. It would survive. The four-leggeds and crawling people would survive. And so would I.

My drive home that evening was magnificent. I never became complacent about nature's mountain beauty. At night the moon sheds its spectral beams down over the heavily forested hills. The looming mountains are ever silhouetted against the silvery light of the low moon. And if you were fortunate enough to desire to see the bare essence of the living mountains, you could slightly alter your consciousness and view the pale blue of the mountain's naked aura—ever proof of the spirit of all living things.

At times such as this, when my spirit would meld with that of the mountains', I never wanted to leave them. Going home to harsh artificial lights and the stiff man-made articles of the house was a grave letdown. There have been nights when I simply wanted to stay within the pure arms of nature. I have, in fact, done just that, because an autumn mountain night is peace for my weary soul. It is there where I softly tread between the pines, and just beside the meandering stream, I reverently reach out and humbly touch the waiting hand of God.

Eyes
Searching

Wide red eyes searched the breadth
of the skies.
They searched the length of the lands.
Silently they kept watch.

The time flew by. I couldn't believe that the week had slipped into my past so quickly. I'd been busy juggling the routine running of an active household with my writings, which was no mean feat. There were several important activities involving the girls that I had to attend. Aimee needed a ride to a horse training class and Sarah needed to be picked up from her friend's house who lived up in the mountains. I seemed to be working around the clock doing these chores and typing during the day and sitting up writing until two or three in the morning. It's no wonder that my week flashed by like a train speeding across the lonesome prairie.

And so Saturday arrived bright and beautiful. And I once again made my habitual journey up into the Pike National Forest. This regal day had successfully captured my spirit. And I was strongly tempted to drive past No-Eyes' turn-off to spend the entire day in precious solitude. Yet, I knew that I must make that decisive turn. I knew someone very dear to me was waiting. I was expected.

The fine morning was scoured by the warm sunshine. I was not greeted by the clouded shadows as was the case of last weekend. Perhaps I could con the old one into a woodland walk today. There were many such times when my lessons were conducted outside in the open air. As I thought back on those specific days, I remembered what a difficult time I had concentrating on the old woman's words. I would let my mind wander amid the carefree character of the nature beings around me and No-Eyes would have to pull out her mental willow stick to discipline her wayward student. When the lessons were moved outside, my classroom became a boundless playground for my happy spirit. I grinned at the comical thought of those times. And I knew that to suggest such a thing to my demanding teacher now, would simply be out of the question. Still.

I pulled up and raced to the cabin.

No-Eyes had her door open and I peered inside. She nearly knocked me over in her rush to get out. "Summer get way today," she blurted exasperatedly.

My eyes widened. "We'll be outside?"

"Humph! I gonna first see how long this gonna last," she wagged into my face.

I was so happy that she consented to have my lesson outside. I figured she thought it wouldn't be long before my mind wandered elsewhere and she'd have to resort to the disciplinary action of moving the classroom back into the mentally stifling confines of the cabin. I was going to try very hard not to have that spirit-binding thing happen.

No-Eyes pulled the multi-colored blanket tighter about her slender form and descended the crude wooden steps.

I had naturally thought that we were going to be sitting on the old branch chairs in her front yard. I anxiously buzzed past her to pull them out of the chilling shadows and into the warm morning sunlight.

Her sharp voice crackled through the mountain stillness. "What you think you doing?"

I froze in place. "I was just setting us up so. . . ."

Her crooked walking stick repeatedly pounded the ground like an out-of-control pile driver. "Get over here!" she barked. "We not gonna sit like two warts on toad! We gonna go in woods today."

Her words fluttered my heart. This day was going to be almost enjoyable I thought as I hurried to her side.

The old one's mind sunk into a well of observation. And when her thoughts had been verified, she boldly cautioned her rambunctious student. "Summer gonna listen today! Summer not be out for joy day!"

"Yes, ma'am!" I shot back trying to suppress my snicker.

Sensing the insubordination, she swiftly spun around and shook her well-used stick at me. "No-Eyes *warn* Summer." She tried to be stern, but she couldn't retain the tight grin that began to lift the wrinkled cheeks.

I warmly smiled back. "You just *think* you're tough. I know you too well to believe phoney threats like that."

"Humph!" she mumbled with dancing eyes that belied her sternness.

We walked down the hill and entered the sun-touched forest. It wasn't long before she called class to order. "This day we gonna speak 'bout what new Phoenix see when eyes looking 'round."

"All right," I replied, reining in my concentration.

She deftly prodded the stoney ground with her staff. She knew exactly where she was going, for she had been sightlessly treading these deep woods for years. "When newborn Phoenix have head out, when he be aware 'nough, he gonna open up red eyes and he gonna look 'round up into sky. He gonna look 'round over all lands, over all waters. He gonna see peoples die. He gonna hear peoples cry."

I picked up a straight branch that had fallen and used it as my own hiking stick. "No-Eyes, what is the Phoenix going to see?"

"I gonna get to that stuff." She cocked her head and listened intently. "Hear the winged people?"

"Yeah," I replied squinting up through the filtered sunlight to where a mountain bluebird perched.

"They meant to fly. They no have stuff go wrong. They know where they go. They fly 'cause Great Spirit give them wings. Summer, peoples not meant to fly in air like the winged people." She slowly shook her head. "Peoples make bad stuff. They fly in bad stuff. Stuff go all bad, peoples fall out of sky—back on ground where they meant to be anyways. Winged people belong in sky. Peoples no belong in sky anyways."

"No-Eyes, people have built wonderful airplanes. Most often they are very safe machines."

"Nope. People make machines to fly. People make time go more fast with sky machines. People go ahead too much, too fast, 'cause of sky machines."

"Oh sure, that's true," I agreed kicking at a shiny piece of mica that had mirrored a sun ray, "but would you have us still using horses?"

She tossed my flip remark over in her mind. "Maybe so." Carefully she stepped over a new-fallen tree branch.

"And also oil lanterns and woodstoves and backhouses?"

"Maybe."

"No-Eyes, there wouldn't be any more trees left then. I don't think you thought about that."

"Humph! What so! No-Eyes *always* think stuff out." Her ebony eyes shifted toward me. "More No-Eyes can say for somebody else I know. What 'bout sun power, water and the power of wind? Huh, Summer? What 'bout all stuff like that? What 'bout energy from Earth Mother's powerful magnet circle?"

"Well yes, but. . . ."

"No buts! No-Eyes teach Summer not to look only in straight lines. No-Eyes all time teach Summer to look 'round corners." She sighed and we walked on. "Summer, peoples gone too far too fast. They gone too fast in wrong direction. They miss right road way back in time."

I agreed with that and I told her so. As far as power was concerned, the scientists were certainly way off the intended track. That made me think of the nuclear plants that were an abomination to the Earth Mother.

"We gonna talk 'bout that stuff some other day. That be part of all new future stuff."

"Nuclear plants?"

"What *left* of stuff like that," she finalized.

Silence.

We veered off the well-troddened path onto one of her more infrequently used ones. She held out her hand for mine. And we hiked a ways in solitude.

The weight of our prolonged silence began to unnerve me. I sought diversion. And the enchanting sights and sounds of my class-room quickly drew me into their hypnotic place in time. I physically continued walking beside my teacher, but mentally and spiritually I was joining another aspect of my world.

Chipmunks skittered nervously in and out of the lush under-growth. The brilliant blue of the mountain bluebird caught my eye and I watched it delicately flit from one aspen branch to another. And the tender sunlight had a mystical way of transforming the golden fragile leaves into translucent pieces of stained glass that reflected a kal-eidoscope of colors through the woodland tunnels of the arched firs and pines.

Behind my eyes I sensed the familiar light-headedness. My consciousness was involuntarily beginning to rise into that initial stage of alpha. I had previously promised myself that I wouldn't allow that to happen today, so I made an effort to lower back into myself. When I turned to my observant teacher, I immediately corrected my truancy. "What were you saying about the airplanes? What did you mean by that?"

The wise one narrowed her eyes as much to say that it was about time I came back down to the classroom, yet she didn't utter a word of admonishment to me about it. She cleverly preferred to ignore my bad behavior by addressing my question. "Phoenix see bad falls. He see planes fall to earth. Many, many fall. Some hit in sky, then fall. Some fall tiny way before they even up in sky."

"What causes these planes to fall?"

"No mystery stuff here. Bad stuff gonna come with all moving machines. That all."

"Major accidents are going to start happening with planes, right?"

"That so, Summer," she admitted in a tone that clearly implied there was more.

"But not *just* with planes," I hedged.

"That so too. Long time ago, No-Eyes be on train. That be time No-Eyes come to here from Red Mountains of Minnesota. Now I no go home that way. Trains not safe! Many bad, bad accidents with trains gonna go on." She lowered her voice. "Strange accidents."

"And buses? Buses take people all across the country too."

"Nope. Summer no get on bus."

"No-Eyes," I gently tried to explain, "people have to have means of traveling. They can't walk everywhere they need to go."

"No matter. That bad too even."

"Walking?" I whispered incredulously.

"Yup. Bad stuff happen to peoples walking too."

Silence.

Tap. Tap. Her stick struck a new obstacle that blocked the narrow pathway.

"I'll get that." I rolled the large granite rock out of her way. We continued strolling into a more dense part of the forest.

"No-Eyes?"

"Yup?"

"It won't be safe to ride a plane, train or bus, will it."

"Nope."

"Nor a car, or the subway, or a monorail, or a motorcycle or a bike."

"That right."

"And it won't be safe to even walk across the street."

"Summer got picture now."

"So, at some time in the future, all forms of transportation will be subjected to freak accidents."

"Yup."

"And the incidence of these freak travel accidents will increase as time goes on."

"That about it all right."

"Why is that? What is going to make all forms of travel so dangerous?"

"Summer forget lesson many months ago? Summer no remember what No-Eyes say 'bout Earth Watchers who no more keep stuff from happening?"

I was duly embarrassed. "Yes, I remember that. You told me

about how they have always favorably interfered with accidents and negative weather systems to prevent mass deaths. But that now they're letting humanity make its own unaware errors. You said that most accidents occur because of the gross unawareness in man's conscious mind. And you also said that it's time the Earth Watchers have to let the people see how careless they have been all along."

She nodded. "That what No-Eyes mean when I say winged people know where they go. They not have machine stuff to go bad. They no can make mistakes 'cause they meant to fly all time anyways. They not need sky machine that go bad. They not need to repair, to fix."

"Mmm," I moaned pensively. "Then perhaps many of the major accidents can possibly be prevented if the machinery involved is checked out regularly and repaired with care."

"Maybe," came the singular word that clearly lacked conviction. "Most gonna happen anyways."

I didn't see the logic. "But why? If people are more careful and conscientious, why wouldn't that prevent a lot of the accidents?"

She was understanding of my hopefulness. "People too busy for time. They in much hurry all times. Peoples no make important time for aware stuff. They too lazy for that."

I held onto my piece of straw. "But if they were *made* aware of that, if they could *see* that they needed to take the time to be more aware, wouldn't that help?"

"Nope," came the sinker.

"I don't get this," I frowned.

"Peoples never gonna learn. It too late anyways. People love lazy path. Peoples be dumb, that all."

Silence. She was perfectly right. Most people would prefer opting for the easier way to do everything. It appeared to be a common trait. Because of the adverse trials connected with my search, this sort of laziness was incomprehensible to me, yet I saw the damaging evidence of it everywhere. And no amounts of forewarning would prevail to alter it. People don't accept the hard aspects of life, the more difficult choices, until they see it to be too late and, only in retrospect, do they attempt to effect a change, but they are unsuccessful—it's just too late.

"No-Eyes, I never cared for planes before, now I know I won't ever get on one again. I always feared them—not the flying, because I really enjoyed the actual flight, but what I feared was the falling."

"That be so funny!" she twittered behind her hand.

Her sudden giggles took me by surprise. "I didn't mean it to be funny! I was serious!"

Snicker. Snicker. "No-Eyes know that. That what make it

so funny."

And I had to chuckle at the sight of her toothless mirth.

My friend sat down to rest on a large boulder, placed the walking stick across her lap and motioned for me to sit next to her. She allowed a deep sigh to escape. "Summer, it be too bad peoples no can see stuff. It be too, too bad."

"Yeah, I know." I made intricate mandalas in the dusty dirt with my stick.

The sun was high in the sky. We enjoyed its welcomed warmth on our faces.

Nearby, an elk stood statue-still—watching, testing the air. No-Eyes immediately sensed its heavy presence and sent out her powerful psyche to greet it. The magnificent creature cocked its regal head and took a cautious step forward. The woman was deep into the delicate moment.

I froze for fear of making a minute movement that would startle our innocent friend away. I could feel the strong electricity that No-Eyes was emitting. And it was charging the air with high intensity voltage. We remained motionless. The animal boldly stepped full out from behind the dense forestline. Again he cocked his massive head. I could feel the forceful current of the old woman's efforts. The animal again took a furtive step toward us. My heart was wildly drumming within the confines of my ribs. I sent waves of friendly and loving thoughts to the curious four-legged person. He became braver. His ingrained fear had vanished. He was so close! Then, within a twitch of an owl's eye, he leaped from view. I released a deep tension-filled breath. And No-Eyes sighed softly. "He be nice one."

"What happened though? You were doing so good with him."

"Summer not be aware," came the cryptic whisper.

I searched the foliage near the forestline and saw the stealthy low crouch of a coyote. "That wouldn't attack the elk!"

"That startle elk! That still mean danger to him."

"Too bad."

"That all part of mountain life. The mighty come. They give notice of you. They share for some silent minute with you. Then they be gone. That way. That be wild nature way."

"Too bad people don't develop their senses like the four-leggeds."

"Yup. That like peoples we been speakin' 'bout."

I became melancholy. "No-Eyes, why does it have to be that way? Why are people not more aware?"

"They just lazy, Summer. That all. No more good reason than that."

"Couldn't it also be karmic? What if all their past lives were spent

37

in laziness, procrastination, couldn't that be an explanation for their laziness in this life?"

"What so?"

"Well, that could be one explanation."

"That be *no* explanation! Last life, many last lifes not be good reason to not fix it, balance it, in this life, see?"

I did see, reluctantly. "I guess."

"No-Eyes know Summer see. Summer just looking 'round for excuse for dumb peoples."

Silence.

As we listened to the nonstop chatter of the scampering squirrels, each of us was lost in our private musings. I wondered at the great amount of unaware people I saw around me everyday. Didn't they realize that there were great things in the offing? I saw no physical evidence of preparation, physical or spiritual. Oh, I knew of separate groups of mountain folks who believed and were taking every opportunity to physically prepare for the bleak future, but on the whole, everyone appeared to be obsessed with worry over the most trivial matters. I found this incredibly difficult to accept. The general unawareness of the masses made them look like mindless robots living out their individual lives with blinders on. I thought about the times when I'd overheard people idly comment on the strange occurrences of this or that, yet nobody was ever aware enough to connect the strange occurrences together. Nobody bothered to fit the puzzle pieces of the signs together. Nobody was aware enough to see the entire picture for what it represented.

"Yup. That right, Summer."

I teasingly poked her ribs. "Why you little minx! Don't you know it's not spiritual to spy on another person's thoughts?"

"Summer not be just other person here. Summer be No-Eyes' student. Summer be No-Eyes' friend."

She was amazing. I hugged her tightly. She knew I never cared if she wanted to "listen in" on me. Besides, I knew that she was ever of the purest intentions. A wise spiritual student automatically knows that they could never hide anything from their teacher, so why even try? I learned much about myself by having No-Eyes analyze my personal thoughts, my thinking process. When nothing is private, when all is out in the open, that is when the real learning takes place. And believe me, it's quite a harrowing experience, one that is invaluable.

"It be nice day here," she commented contentedly.

"Yeah, it really is."

She bent her head as if she were searching the ground. "It be special nice with Summer here."

Compliments or comments that revealed her deep feelings toward me were few and far between, in fact, they were downright rare. When they were verbalized they touched me deeply. And now her words swelled my sensitive heart. I laid my hand on her arm. "I love you too, No-Eyes."

The sun reached down and gently touched the two women in the forest clearing. And a royal elk peered out between the thick squaw-berry bushes. He picked up something new wafting on the wind. He curiously craned his neck forward and lifted his snout up into the air to flare his nostrils wide as the crisp autumn breeze carried the scent of friendship that emanated from the rosy aura of the two women sitting in the clearing.

Listening

And the newborn cocked his
iridescent head.
He cocked his head and listened
to the wretched cries of humanity.

Sunday morning dawned bright with a special clarity to the air that reflected the mirrored image of the previous day. And I was glad that my beautiful mountain autumn days were holding their own warm brilliance before they fell victim to the biting and bitter cutlass that winter wielded so wildly about.

As I drove through the lonely roads, I thought about the discussion Bill and I had had the night before. I had shared all that my wise friend had told me. Like myself, Bill was surprised at the extent the freak accidents would take. We talked about the slim probability of people learning to become aware. And we agreed that there just was not time for them to develop the constant concentrated awareness that was so important in the future.

Lessons in awareness were much more difficult than one might expect. It takes more than a simple centering of the conscious mind. It takes a form of being able to equally split the consciousness between all the senses, thereby bringing the mind into a totally crystal-clear awareness of all outside stimuli entering the physical body. It is clearly evident as I speak with people, that they are not aware enough, they are not centering on my words. Most often, their mind is being flooded with things they are trying to remember to say. Many times they will mentally be off in some other world. I can see it in their eyes. I can easily read their distracting thoughts. People really don't listen well, if indeed, they listen at all.

And, Bill and I reached the rather obvious conclusion. We had to concur with the old woman. Nobody was going to avoid their accidents through a warning or a speedy crash course in awareness. So we felt rather at odds and completely helpless to intervene in any positive way. This type of realization was always especially difficult for us to accept, to deal with. We were here together to spread the deep spiritual wisdom and foresight of our friend, No-Eyes, yet when we reached an area where none of our efforts could effect a positive alteration, we were at an impasse with ourselves. Yes, we could warn, yet what good is the warning if no active steps can be taken to avert the negative outcome? We were always informed of our purpose to give out information and warnings. Ours was not to alter anything. Ours was to simply aid anyone we could and allow the recipient to take it from there. There have been times when the temptation to urge a person out of a wrong direction was so incredibly strong, however, we must forever restrain this urge because then we are crossing the very fine line between helping an individual and that of interfering with their free will.

The free will should be one of an individual's most prized possessions. This is an elementary spiritual concept. If we were to urge and warn a person continually, or if we were to continually point out their errors and future downfalls, we would be grossly affecting that person's right to choose. An individual's free will is the one aspect of their spirit that brings about that individual's spiritual advancement, or lack of same. It is vitally imperative that each person retain a strong free will. When people are led around and constantly told which paths to take, they are not advancing themselves; they are no more than robots.

Spiritual advancement comes through the tiresome exercise of the free will. Spritual advancement comes through the correct choices of that free will and through the long suffering of the physical *because* of those correct choices. Spiritual advancement is not a paved road. It is literally strewn with dead-ends, high walls, and dark pitfalls. It is the trail of long suffering and tears, disappointments, and rejections. You inherently know in your heart if you are walking the trail to advancement or if you are casually strolling down the shaded sidewalk of easy street.

Another reason we were warned to never actively direct an individual's life was because we would then be pointedly interfering with their private karma. Each person must eventually attempt to balance out their karma alone. Yes, we could tell an individual precisely what he needs to accomplish in order for him to successfully achieve his all important end. However, aren't we then shortening his path? Is that not an active interference by us? Many people need to come into their *own* realization of their purpose here on earth. If we were to reveal those key realizations, then we would be actively interfering with that individual's karma. Some things are not meant to be revealed. Some things are out of our hands to share and to help with. And the increased incidents of freak accidents was one of those things. We accept what cannot be changed. That has been a great part of our own learning. A difficult lesson to accept—but accept we must.

I pulled up onto the familiar road and shut off the tired, old engine. I remained in the truck and stared at my home-away-from-home. To me, that centennial time-worn cabin was synonymous with love. It was such a meager dwelling for one such as my scholarly friend. She should have an easier life. She should have a furnace and electricity, a flush toilet, and better furniture. Yet, all those conveniences would only serve to change her lifestyle. She couldn't be altered. She was perfectly content with the way things were. She fit perfectly within the framework of the cracked log walls of her small cabin. It was home to her. And it was home to me.

I walked up the hill and took heightened delight in autumn's crisp essence. Smoke snaked lazily up from her stone chimney in friendly wavering curls. And I broke into a run to greet the person within the welcoming cabin.

"'Morning, No-Eyes!" I excitedly greeted.

"'Mornin', Summer." She was replacing her wooden breakfast bowl into her cupboard. I took my serape off and was about to join her in the kitchen when she voiced other orders. "We go in there," she said pointing to the living room.

"Okay," I said sitting down on the couch.

She shuffled out of the kitchen area and pulled her trusty rocker over in front of me.

I playfully teased her. "Sure is a great day out there. S'pose we're not going for a walk . . . are we?"

"Nope."

"Guess two days in a row would be a little too much to expect, huh."

"Yup."

"I was afraid of that."

She rearranged her woven shawl, fidgeted a bit and looked straight into my eyes.

My lesson was beginning and, without another word spoken between us, I knew what she was requiring. I sat upright and stretched out my legs. With hands resting gently on my lap I closed my eyes. I sat in this relaxed position for several minutes until I could detach my

43

mental from my physical. Soon, when I felt as though my entire body was paralyzed, when the nonfeeling of any external physical sensation was evident, I was properly prepared to send up the spirit. My mental energies were centered slightly above my eyes, and gathering a brilliant light within that region, I gently let it raise like a child's balloon. I was out.

No-Eyes was already there, holding out her beautiful hand. And together we drifted through the nebulous dimensions of time. After a while she spoke. "Newborn Phoenix got head out now, Summer. He gonna take much time listening now. Summer know what newborn Phoenix gonna hear?"

"Plane crashes and trains derailing."

"Nope. He gonna hear guns. He gonna hear bodies hit ground. He gonna turn mighty head and hear peoples moan in great sickness."

Silence.

"We gonna go see what make sounds Phoenix gonna hear."

Drifting.

I wasn't at all enthused about actually making this mystical journey into her ugly painting of the future. Yet, she always devised the most effective lessons. Who was I to question her methods or refuse cooperation? Indeed, next to her, who was I?

We drifted through a most intensely palatable darkness. A darkness that bulged and sagged with its own deep breathing surrounded us. All of life pulsed with an essence of energy. And this darkness we were drifting through also possessed a pulsing life of its own.

I whispered to the old wizened one. I whispered because it didn't seem appropriate to speak out in a normal voice. "Where are we?"

She answered in her usual tone. "Summer not know?"

I winced from the loudness that echoed from her voice. "No," I whispered again.

A loud cackling laugh rent the stillness. "Why Summer whispering like some child up to no good stuff?"

I furtively glanced about. "I'm whispering like a child because I think I should be whispering. I don't feel comfortable talking any louder than this. No-Eyes, I'm very uncomfortable right now."

She squeezed a bit on my hand. "You not in some library. You not in some big fancy church. Summer can talk up. Summer not have to whisper here."

I still couldn't bring myself to speak up. It was against my better judgement. And I continued our conversation in lowered tones. "I still feel terribly uncomfortable." I peered through the darkness. "I feel as though I'm being watched."

"Silly woman," she grinned. "Maybe No-Eyes name you all wrong. Maybe No-Eyes change name to Silly Woman, maybe even to Scared Woman." She giggled at her own wry humor.

I saw nothing funny about the dark heaviness that surrounded us. "I'm not laughing, No-Eyes. Do you hear me laughing?"

She tried to be more serious. "No-Eyes sorry, but Summer be so funny anyways."

"Thanks a lot. Now tell me why I feel eyes on my back?" I insisted.

She ominously shifted her ebony eyes. "Eyes always be on back. This no different stuff."

"You know what I mean. Stop playing games."

She sighed. "Summer not be fun no more. Summer need to think, that all." She became silent so that I would do my expected thinking.

I held tightly onto my secure lifeline. The comfort of her hand gave me the needed reassurance to relax my fears and to gather together some logical thoughts. As soon as the fears fell away I became aware of other etheric forms around us, there were hundreds of them.

I adjusted my awareness and discovered that we were drifting along an avenue of some type. And the other forms were as varied as the fieldflowers that grew in my mountain meadows.

People, human people, drifted in our direction and also in the opposite direction. But many other intelligent lifeforms were also passing to and fro along this mystical byway. Some of the foreign forms were familiar to me, yet many more were entirely strange. They were conversing with one another like ordinary people out on a Sunday afternoon stroll through the park. My fears vanished as I relaxed with the awareness of this busy byway we were on. Then I silently chuckled at the humorous sight of one unusual lifeform.

Suddenly my hand was jerked hard in a disciplinary manner. "Summer be impolite! No-Eyes teach Summer better manners than that!"

I was ashamed, and I think that if I had had a solid physical form, I would've blushed. I lowered my head. "I'm sorry."

"Summer should be! That being have more brains than whole earth people put all together. Summer not *ever* laugh at other beings."

"I know. I said I was sorry. It's just that he suddenly struck me as being funny."

"Summer need to keep all feelings like that quiet. No can let others see that stuff, see?"

I nodded. "Where was that being from? Can you tell me that?"

"Could, but Summer not understand anyways. He be from other universe far away. Earth peoples be dumb, they not even know 'bout all stuff in Milky Way. They not even know 'bout stuff in own universe. How they gonna know 'bout stuff in *other* places? Earth peoples be so *dumb*. They think they in *only* universe. They so dumb all times. They not even believe in *other* places!"

"Yeah well...."

"*No* yeah well! They *dumb*, that all!"

She was shouting at me and the travelers along the byway turned heads. She would forever get overwhelmingly angry and worked up whenever our discussions touched upon the lacking knowledge of modern science.

I attempted to soothe her heated temper. "No-Eyes, come on, we both know all that, but...."

"*Everybody* know all that! Look! *Look*, Summer! *See*? *They* all know too!" The frail woman's spirit was hopping around pointing to the other lifeforms that were trying to ignore the wild rantings of her highly inflammable emotions that had ignited.

I was embarrassed as I looked around and saw many of the beings making strange sounds that could only be interpreted as sympathy. I nervously smiled, nodded and waved to them as we passed. No-Eyes certainly could be difficult to control when she got this way. I turned back to her and was startled to see several of the alien beings comforting her. There were three of them. I watched in a daze as they slowly drifted right into her being. I could actually distinguish four distinct forms occupying the singular mass of energy space I knew to be No-Eyes. I stood transfixed with amazement as the translucence of the etheric forms caressed and, as I watched, a terrific rosy light began to emit from the group aura. I still held my friend's hand, and as the light pulsed down her arm, it inched up my own. And I found myself crying from the total love and compassion that it carried with it. It warmly consumed my inexperienced spirit.

Then the beings slowly backed away and nodded cordially to me before they continued on their way. No words were ever exchanged. None were needed.

No-Eyes looked deep into my eyes. She was completely tranquilized. "That be love, Summer. That be real love."

We drifted a ways before she spoke again. "Summer figure out stuff yet?"

I was pleased to be able to nod a positive reply.

"Summer not gonna tell?"

I really didn't want to talk just yet. That short bout with real love had so totally enthralled me that I didn't desire to break its intoxicating spell by speaking, and I told her so.

She smiled with understanding. "Summer like that love?"

I nodded. "That was the most beautiful selfless emotion I've ever felt from anyone. Yes, I liked that very much."

The old one pointed to a lone being walking toward us. His pace was exceedingly slow and he was obviously downcast. "Summer like feeling? Summer go show feeling—go give it." She again tilted her head toward the being and then she pulled my hand forward.

I questioningly looked at her as if I needed further approval to go ahead with the suggestion.

She quickly gave that approval. "It okay. Go 'head." She pushed me forward.

I drifted toward the saddened being. He noticed my approach and stood still. I had never done anything like this before and I wasn't quite sure that I could pull off the precise mechanics necessary to accomplish the correct meld of love. I had no way of knowing how to do it. But I felt an intense empathy for this heart-broken etheric being.

I hesitantly drifted closer—closer. And before I realized it, I was completely within the being. I paused, then gave him all the love and sympathy I could muster up. My world was suddenly engulfed in an undulating pink thickness. No-Eyes no longer existed to me. My physical world no longer existed to me. All the passing beings no longer existed. I heard no sounds. I saw no images, only the light of my pure love and deep compassion. And we two separate beings from two separate worlds were one. Together we shared and were consumed within the powerful light of a universal language.

I drifted back. He drifted back. He nodded slowly in appreciation. I nodded back with tears flooding my eyes and I returned to my teacher's side.

She spoke softly. She was aware of my present state of heightened sensitivity. "That not so hard, huh Summer."

Looking down at my feet, I shook my head.

"Seems Summer always have new stuff to learn. Summer never stop learning, that part of life. That great big part of awareness stuff."

"Yeah," I whispered.

"Summer see and do many hard stuff. See? Summer now do easy, good stuff too, even!" She patted my back.

My eyes sought hers. "I wish people on earth could do that. I wish the simple act of giving comfort could be so effortless, so honestly and openly given."

"It is!" she flared with a fiery excitement.

I solemnly shook my head in respectful disagreement. "No it isn't, No-Eyes. People can't feel the suffering of others."

The old one maintained a childlike insistence. "Summer can. People be like Summer."

I thought about how innocent she could be. She couldn't actually comprehend some things. She was so wise, yet when it came to certain human conditions, she was as a small child brimming with unbounded trust and complete belief. "Let's change the subject," I urged out of frustration.

She would have none of my ruse. "We not gonna change no stuff here! Peoples *can* give comfort. Peoples *can* give love. They give like just now!"

At this moment in time I felt sorry for her. "No-Eyes, please," I pleaded.

"No! We gonna talk! Much comfort, much love gonna be needed now, soon. Earth Mother gonna be sad in great pains. Peoples gonna be sad. They cry. They die even. They gonna need all comfort they can get!"

"Well," I eased in, "perhaps the changes will also change the people then. But right now the world is in a tight grip of cold apathy. Everyone turns their heads away from the uncomfortable feelings that suffering brings. Everyone would rather simply look the other way. No-Eyes, nobody wants to get involved with each other anymore. Too many people have built such a hardened shell around themselves that they can't even show what feelings they do have."

"Summer can. They can," she mumbled under her determined breath.

Her stubborn insistence infuriated me. I wasn't going to let her have the final word, even if it was just a mumble under her breath. "No-Eyes! I'm an *empath!* And you *know* that! People aren't *like* me! Do *they* absorb the miseries of the world? Do *they* feel heartsick with the unbelievers? No-Eyes, do *they* let the screams of human suffering consume them until it gets so bad that they have to flee up into the mountains to let out the heavy burden with their soul song?"

Silence.

"Well? *Do* they, No-Eyes?" I shouted while a stinging pricked behind my eyes.

She softened. "I sorry. I not be fair to Summer."

Releasing the tension, I sighed deeply. "I'm sorry too. I didn't mean to make a scene like that. I'm sorry for my outburst."

She shrugged indifferently. "No-Eyes bring that on anyways." She paused a moment before altering the mood. "But No-Eyes see peoples gonna change anyways."

I gave up. "They'll have to, won't they. They'll have no choice but to cling to one another in their grief."

"Yup. That way it gonna be all right." Then she perked up. "So! Summer decide where we be?"

"I think we're on an etheric path of some type, a path that leads into the future."

"Humph. Summer be almost right. Summer be pretty right."

"Almost? Pretty right?"

"This be named Corridor of Time. It not easy way. It not be easy to reach. I know way. I bring Summer. Summer learn way so...."

"Wait a minute," I ordered after getting her drift. "I don't want to come here alone."

"No have to come alone. Summer bring Bill. Summer and Bill love and comfort each other here."

That idea was truly inviting. To bring Bill here and to share that magnificent pink light with him was an almost irresistible temptation. Then I reasoned logically. "But we could join spirits like that *anywhere*." I feigned shock. "You've been trying to *trick* me into bringing him into the Corridor!"

She shrugged sheepishly. "No-Eyes try. Summer too smart. Guess I too good teacher." Her gums gleamed between grinning lips.

"Well, just pat yourself on the back some more!" I teased.

"No-Eyes trick Summer much before—now it not be so easy," she admitted playfully.

And that was a definite compliment. "Thank you for that."

I was beginning to enjoy our footless stroll through the Corridor of Time when the old woman stopped short. I nearly knocked her over—ran through her so to speak. "What's the matter?"

She turned with a solemn expression that underlined the gravity of the moment. "We here, Summer. This be where we gonna leave. We gonna go down now to see what Phoenix hear."

A quick surge lunged through my undefined heart. "I'm ready." I heaved a deep breath and we drifted out of the crowded byway.

The darkness was noticeably less dense now. The moving mass of beings was left behind and all was silent—temporarily.

Down we drifted. And the descent was clearly marked by a sharp awareness of warmer atmosphere. We neared the Earth. And even as distant as we still were, the human cries of desperation and misery were deafening to my acute senses. They rose up through the fine substance of our surroundings and echoed with repeating reverberations.

I clapped my hands over my etheric ears and I motioned to No-Eyes that I could hear no more—I could go no farther.

The wise one mystically passed her hand over my head and gently pulled away my tense hands.

Silence. Sweet, precious silence. She had compassionately removed the horrible sounds of humans in the throes of terrible suffering.

I found the action to be selective, in that I could still hear her and only certain things that would be necessary, yet the audible screams were successfully blocked out. She reached for my hand and led me downward into the future world, down into the cesspool of human misery known as Earth.

I extracted a measured amount of comfort in my friend's warm hand. I trusted her implicitly. Side by side, we descended upon the Earth Mother. The old one spoke to me as she searched out our first stop. "We gonna go to different places. We gonna see what Phoenix hear from different places." She had located our initial destination, and we veered off to the right.

As we approached a crowded amusement park, the gaiety of the fun-loving people was most predominant as being my first impression. We joined the milling crowds. And although the reception of my audio sense had been tampered with, I could well imagine the loud, garish sounds of the park. We passed the laughing children who were gleefully riding up, down and around on their brightly-painted ponies and elephants. I loved watching little children at play and I smiled at No-Eyes who quickly returned the shared sentiment.

We wandered past the busy arcade and momentarily paused to observe a young man making valiant attempts to win a giant teddy bear for his anxious sweetheart. The unfortunate man wasn't faring well at all, in fact, he was down to his last remaining two quarters. Then, as if he had cast a magical spell, he easily knocked over all the weighted bottles. And he beamed with pride as he handed the large pink bear to his girl.

We walked away.

I couldn't have helped noticing the slight movement my companion had made with her hand just before the young man became so proficient with his last set of sandbags. "Why'd you do that back there?"

She dropped her jaw in incredulous shock. "Do what?"

I grinned from ear-to-ear at the sight of her exaggerated pretention. "Direct those sandbags."

"Sandbags?"

Shaking my head, I waved my hand at her. "Oh forget it. I saw what you did. You don't have to admit it if you don't care to. I saw what I saw, though."

She acted like a little girl who had been caught in the act of committing a no-no. "Summer not s'posed to see some stuff."

That was ridiculous. "Why not?"

"'Cause I not s'posed to interfere like that," she reasoned a bit sheepishly.

50

"Then why did you?" I questioned like a prodding parent.

"Peoples gonna have many bad days comin'. Things be bad 'nough. No-Eyes just make tiny bit of happy, that all." Then she shrugged and smiled through eyes that danced with mischief. "Besides, that game stuff all fixed anyways."

I nodded in agreement. "Still, that was a noble thing for you to do. I figured those were probably your reasons."

She jerked my hand. "Why Summer ask if Summer already know answers?"

"No-Eyes, remember when I asked you that very same question during our first days together? Do you recall your answer?"

"Yup, No-Eyes remember. We gonna move on now."

We cleared the arcade area and approached the midway of rides. Dozens of mammoth rides circled, tilted, swooped and spun. The riders were laughing and screaming in delight. Considering the gravity of our purpose, I couldn't imagine why we were here in this park of happy people. We passed clowns that tumbled and clowns that sadly mimed. We passed groups of jugglers, sideshow bakers, and hackers of tinsel souvenirs. We passed little children happily eating cotton candy bundles that were bigger than they were. And I chuckled at one extremely overweight gentleman who was daintily consuming a foot-long hot dog, all the while totally oblivious to the steady stream of bright mustard that dribbled down his great beer belly. No-Eyes suddenly jerked hard on my hand.

I quickly replied to the action. "I know," I admitted, "I shouldn't have laughed at him."

The old one's head shook. "He be funny all right. It be okay. But now we look at *that!*" She spun us around and pointed to the enormous monster of a double ferris wheel. The people were being loaded on. If I had been in the physical, just looking up to the top of that thing would've made me weak in the knees. I couldn't stand heights.

We watched as the excited riders were carefully loaded and buckled in their seats. The operator pulled the lever forward. The giant ride creaked and groaned as the twin wheels began to circle past each other.

I looked at No-Eyes. She was watching intently as I studied her anxious face. Slowly, she turned to me. And I froze from the chill of her eyes. We both returned our attention to the huge ride. It appeared to have swayed slightly. Then, a main support bulged and snapped. What we then witnessed was an unimaginable tragedy.

People were helplessly flung through the air, some still strapped securely into their runaway seats. Their mouths were stretched wide in horrifying screams as they plunged to their certain deaths. The entire ferris wheel fell over sideways into three other moving rides, adding more innocent people to the total death number. The hideous scene was grotesquely gory. I couldn't watch anymore and I shut my eyes while pleadingly tugging on No-Eyes' arm.

She tapped my shoulder. "It okay now, Summer. My voice all Summer can hear."

I remained paralyzed with my eyes tightly shut behind clutching hands. "I know. I always could hear your voice, but I don't want to *see* anymore of that horrid scene!"

"Summer, it all gone. Look."

I snuck a peak through two fingers. All was blackness once more. My relief was evident as I sighed before speaking. "No-Eyes, that was the most sickening thing I've ever witnessed." I felt tears welling, burning, brimming.

"No! Summer not feel that stuff here!"

"God! I can't *help* it!" And I began to cry.

The old woman put her arm around me and entered my trembling being. She drew up my sorrow. She was a human magnet that withdrew all my empathy. And she compassionately replaced it with a sweet and beautiful peace. Together, our spirits remained interlocked until the substitution was complete. And when we separated, I squeezed her hand in heartfelt gratitude.

"Summer no can have feelings like that here. We gonna see more bad stuff. Spirit no can be sad, no can be sponge for what it see—feel."

"Thanks to you, I'll be okay now." I mentally faltered as the vivid images of the previous scene replayed across the screen of my mind. "That terrible accident, what does it signify? Wasn't that just a...a freak accident?" The reality speared into the forefront of my mind. "Oh God, No-Eyes, you mean things like *that* are going to be happening too?"

She nodded sorrowfully. "Yup. Many more rides of fun, gonna go bad even."

"But why?" I whined with a voice full of painful empathy.

She raised an eyebrow. "Why?"

"I see," I admitted sadly. "It's all part of people's lack of awareness. It's all a little part of the grand unleashing of the Earth Watcher's protection." I looked away into the darkness. "But it seems so mean," I moaned softly.

"Mean? Mean you say? It not be mean for peoples to realize how careless, how unaware they be all 'long. Summer, when Earth Watchers always be helping to cover up peoples mistakes, peoples no learn!"

That had been the most heartless, inhumane concept I'd ever heard coming from her lips. It went against all my values. It stabbed at my sensitivity. I was angered. "*That's* no way to teach anything!" I flared.

Yet, the experienced wise one remained calm and unruffled by her enraged student. "Please, Summer, try to understand stuff here. Remember way back many days, when we talk 'bout how Great Spirit gonna let stuff go, how *He* gonna let peoples see mistakes, how *He* gonna give long, long rope?"

The sharp cutting edge of the concept suddenly tempered into the sword of Justice. Then it dawned on me that God was indeed letting His people make their own decisions, realizations, and mistakes without any outside protective force involved. I calmed. "Yes, I remember."

"Good. Now we gonna go see some other place. No-Eyes gonna show Summer more ways people gonna act after Earth Watchers stop protecting them." She quickly glanced around and we were speeding off again.

This time we lowered into a most pleasant scene. We began strolling down one of the beautifully peaceful streets of a middle American town. The large, trim homes were set back from the street and were pleasingly fronted with neatly manicured, green lawns. The trees gracefully towered together forming a natural wavering arch over the street. Bright geraniums and petunias were carefully planted around the home fronts. Children playfully romped in the wide yards. Birds chirped. The neighborly postman whistled as he waved to his friendly customers. And a milk truck slowly puttered its leisurely way toward us.

I was completely taken in by the pastoral little neighborhood of the town. In the physical, I had driven through many just like it. I had always admired them, just as I did this one. "This is so peaceful," I whispered leaning close to my friend.

The old one gave me one of her cryptic questioning looks and my heart took a stomach-churning nose dive. I reviewed the perfect setting again. Nothing out of the ordinary appeared in evidence. Not one single thing seemed wrong. I gave No-Eyes a dubious look.

And she brought up a basic tenent. "No stuff *ever* be like they *look*. We gonna stay here minute more. We gonna watch."

A gentle breeze wafted through the trees. Bees buzzed in and around the multi-colored blossoms. A lazy collie yawned and stretched out on a shaded porch.

I watched, but saw only the everyday activities of an ordinary small town's summer morning.

The milk truck neared, slowed and stopped. The deliveryman hesitated within the cab, then cheerfully stepped out with a wire basket filled with an assortment of dairy products swinging from his arm. He hummed a tune as he skipped up the wide steps of a red brick colonial. I saw nothing unusual, nothing like what No-Eyes had wanted me to see. I watched.

Soon the handsome milkman exited the house and continued to hum as he waved to a passing woman pushing a stroller. They cordially exchanged pleasantries before parting for their separate ways. And No-Eyes again gave me that spine-tingling stare of hers.

I quickly looked around the neighborhood for something bad happening.

Nothing.

The wise one shook her head in mild disgust. "Summer see, but Summer not see."

I took a frantic survey again in all directions. Not one blasted thing was amiss! I was baffled by her statement. "See *what?*"

"See *this!*" She yanked me into the colonial. We entered the kitchen. My stomach churned. A woman was sprawled on the floor with a steak knife wedged deeply into her chest. Immediately No-Eyes sped us back to the street. Her words came gently. "That be murder, Summer. "That gonna happen much more."

I was bewildered. "But that guy acted so *normal!*"

"Yup. That way it gonna be. Peoples gonna just snap minds. They gonna go crazy. They gonna do much crazy stuff—crazy sudden murder."

That frightened me just knowing that there was a dead woman in that house. It sent chills through me.

No-Eyes sensed the effect and we moved on down the seemingly peaceful street a ways before she halted in front of a white cape cod. I was afraid to look at it so I stared at her instead.

"Go on," she urged, "it just a house."

I didn't believe her for one minute. I hadn't spent these past months in her rigorous training without also learning a great deal about my teacher. And one thing I caught on real quick about was when she was tricking me. This was most definitely one of her clever coverups.

I snuck a hesitant glance at the house and my head crawled. The place was surrounded by a dark undulating aura. Something was very wrong. Something was very amiss within that little innocent looking cottage. "There's *death* all *over* in there!" I blurted with mixed emotions of anger and shock.

Cold eyes met mine. Colder words came. "We go see." And my teacher pulled my hand as we drifted toward the shrouded building.

Oh God, let me survive this lesson, I silently pleaded.

But she had heard. "Summer no need pleas. Summer gonna

help in there."

Oh my *God!*

She led me past the front door and up through the silent house. I felt the heavy presence of more than one spirit—several. We went to the second floor and into a small brightly decorated bedroom. It was a nursery. And in two identical cribs, lay a two-year old boy and girl. They had been suffocated. I was immediately sickened at the wasting of such innocent little lives.

No-Eyes cautioned me. "Summer no judge—yet." Then we crossed the hallway and entered the large bathroom. We didn't have to look further for another body. We never actually saw the mother of the dead twins, but the splatters that still dripped down the glass shower enclosure was evidence enough as to what lay behind it.

I was repulsed and had the strong urge to retch. My spirit wasn't actually capable of such a physical act, but it could clearly feel the emotional sensation of the mind's repulsion. I fled the room. I raced down the stairs and into three waiting lost spirits. Filled with a wild panic, I spun around and looked up for my protector.

She was standing at the top of the stairs. "Go on, Summer," came the chilling order, "go help them."

I reeled back to face the moaning woman. The crying children were clutching onto their mother's legs. I didn't have the faintest idea of how to handle this. In desperation, I shot pleading eyes up at No-Eyes for guidance.

None came. Nothing came but coldness. "Summer do. Summer do stuff alone." And my backup vanished.

My head prickled again as I watched her spirit dissolve. I was left alone with three spirits. What was I supposed to do? What the hell was I supposed to do with them? Then, without another conscious thought, I slowly turned back to the sad spirits and held out my arms.

Taking the cue, they drifted toward me and all four of us completed the love meld of spirits. Their pitiful moans and desolate cries stopped. I pulled back and guided them to the living room where the sun flooded in through antique lace curtains. I uttered only one word to the woman. "Why?"

She began to pace about the bright room. "I had no choices left, no choices at all. My husband was vice president of a big company. He had taken a considerable amount of money from this company over the years, and he was finally caught last month." She wrung her hands. "He's in jail. I had no job. They took everything but this house. What was left for me to do? I tried to find work, but I couldn't make enough to cover the expenses. I didn't know what to do anymore. So I did the only thing left to do."

"You were wrong," I stated flatly.

She halted in midstep. "Wrong? How can you say that? Don't you see," she twitted nervously, "now we can live here and never again have to worry about anything. It's perfect. It's just so perfect."

I raised my voice. "It's *not* perfect! And you *can't* stay here!" I shouted.

She was surprised. "And why not?" she asked haughtily.

I calmed. "Because this is not where you belong anymore, that's why. This is a physical house. It has been built as a comfortable shelter for physical bodies."

A shadow of bewilderment crossed her face. "So?"

"*Look* at yourself! *Look* at those *children!*"

Her eyes searched the room for her little boy and girl. She spotted them just in time before they disappeared through a wall. She turned back to me in shock, then examined her own hands. She hypnotically raised her trembling hands to feel the hard substance of her face. There wasn't any. "Oh *God!* We're *dead!*"

"Don't call on *Him!* You're *dead* all right. You and your kids are as dead as dead can get!"

She was confused. "But, *this* isn't heaven! Where's heaven? Why aren't we in heaven?

"Heaven is within the Being of God. Heaven is only for those with a purified spirit. You have done an unthinkable thing here. You must realize that before we can go on."

She ran through the wall after her children. I rushed to follow and joined her in the next room. She was standing in frozen shock. We watched as the childrens' beautiful guides held their small hands and led them through a tunnel of swirling clouds toward the brilliance beyond.

"They're leaving," she whispered numbly. "Where are they going?"

"To the otherside," I replied softly.

She was mesmerized as she helplessly stared after them. "Are they going to heaven?" asked the trance-like figure.

I placed my arm around her shoulders and led her back into the sunny room. "That depends."

"On what?"

"Don't worry, they'll be in loving hands. They'll be just fine."

We sat in weighted silence while I gave her the opportunity to let her mesmerized state fade. When she looked at me with clear eyes, I continued. "You can't stay here."

"I must. I've done a terrible thing up there." She looked up at the ceiling.

"Other people will come here. Someday others will buy this house and they'll. . . ."

Her eyes flared with fire. "*No!* This is *my* house! *Mine* I tell you, *mine!*"

"You can't *possess* this house! You *can't* possess *anything* anymore! You're *dead!*"

She snapped up her chin in defiance and calmly replied, "I'll simply stay here and clean and. . . ."

"No! No! *No!*"

She sneered down her nose at me. "And just *who* the hell are *you* to tell me otherwise?"

This was real difficult for me. I could see that my present method wasn't getting us anywhere. I stood, raised my arm, and sliced my hand down through the end table. "How are you going to keep your lovely physical house clean if you can't even hold onto a dustcloth?"

Having no logical answer, she merely shrugged.

I tried another line of strategy. "And what about the other people who will live here? They'll be strangers," I softly interjected.

"No!" She shot to her feet. "I'll *not* have *strangers* in *my* house!"

Remaining calm, I attempted to throw in a few wrenches. "But you're dead. And this is a physical place for physical people—living people."

"I'll. . .I'll *scare* them! *That's* what I'll do," she reasoned smuggly, "I'll just scare them all away and then I'll have my house all to myself." She brightened at the cleverness of her idea. "This will be *fun!*" she exclaimed impishly.

Bigger wrenches coming. "And then?" I pushed.

"And then I'll be happy."

"Will you? Who will keep the years of dust from accumulating over everything? Who will prevent your lovely home from falling into decay?"

"Well. . .I can't. . .I can't care about that," she justified.

Then I found the biggest wrench in my bag of tricks. "And nobody will care to live in your dilapidated house. Nobody will ever buy your haunted house. And they'll destroy it. They'll have no recourse but to raze it to the ground."

"Oh God!"

I was finally breaking up some ice. "So then you'll have *no* house. Do you care about this house more than you care for your children?"

"That was real cute," she snapped sarcastically.

"I thought so too, because that's just what you've been telling *me* all this time."

She thought on that. And the ice melted with cries of despair.

I kept up the verbal flow. "Do you want to be with your children or with this house?"

'My children," she sobbed.

"Well then, get going!"

She raised her head with renewed hope. "But how can I go there when I've done such a sinful thing? Don't I *have* to stay here? Aren't I *bound* here by my awful misdeed?"

I compassionately shook my head. "The otherside is for *all* spirits. You'll be loved and helped through your difficulties. There will be others who will show you what you need to do next—what is required to balance out your recent offense."

This spirit reality information was completely foreign to her former beliefs. She needed better clarification. "I won't be judged and sent to *hell?*"

I smiled at her. "Oh you'll be judged all right, but you certainly won't be sent to hell. I can absolutely promise you that won't happen. *You're* going to judge *yourself!*"

She tossed this new concept over in her mind. She had made her decision. "How do I do this? How do I get to there from here?"

"Then you don't want to stay here in this house?"

"When I can be with my children? No way!" Her tears were brimming.

"What are you waiting for, let's go!"

Then, as if an esoteric door opened, as if her desire mystically touched off a spiritual button, we were suddenly joined by another presence. The woman's personal guide presented himself to her. He wrapped his comforting arms about her and led her toward the bright tunnel that had formed. At the end, standing within the brilliant illumination, were her two children.

They called to her. They sounded far away. "Mama? *Mama!*"

The woman forgot about her helpful guide and she raced through the whirling tunnel. "My babies! My *babies!* Mama's *coming!*"

The gentle man in the forest green robe stood at the tunnel entrance and watched his charge run to her home. He turned to me and gave me a thankful nod before walking through to the otherside.

I felt tired. But I was also proud of myself. The woman was the first spirit I had to send along its way. I sighed and swung around to search for No-Eyes. I didn't have to look far. She was standing directly behind me.

"Well?" I asked with a certain amount of puffed up pride. "How'd I do?"

"Okay," she answered with a shrug.

What a let down. "Just okay? That's it?"

"Summer do fine, for spirit work. Someday Summer gonna need to clear places in *physical* reality."

"What?"

"Summer be hard of hearing all sudden? I say Summer and Bill gonna clear places in Colorado, clear places of mixed up and restless spirits of Indian and white peoples. Summer do that in physical life."

"When? Where?"

"That other day stuff. That not for now. We go now." She dissolved.

And that was that. I was so proud of myself for clearing the house of the woman's poor confused spirit. I felt sure that No-Eyes was going to agree that I had handled the new situation well. But then, I didn't do things to receive her pats on the back. I did them to learn. And learn I did.

I too left the house and found her sitting on a shaded curb. "Well, now what?"

"Sit down," she ordered, "it coming."

I sat next to her and watched an old lady cross the street. Before I knew it, a car had taken the corner at break-neck speed and struck the woman down. I stood.

No-Eyes roughly pulled me back down. "Summer no can do stuff. She dead. See?"

I watched a crowd of people gather around the accident scene. And there, directly above the crumpled body, was the beautiful etheric form of the woman. She reached up her hand. Another grabbed it, and she too was rapidly whisked through to the other dimension known as the afterlife. "That was so fast!" I exclaimed.

"Yup. She be ready."

The ambulance arrived and the team of dedicated paramedics worked frantically on her. They made a valiant attempt to recall the life of the bleeding and broken woman. She couldn't hear though. She didn't care. She was already far away.

No-Eyes got to her feet. "We got two more places to see."

I followed her into a yellow ranch house. There was a lot of activity. Children played. Dogs ran about. The father was refinishing the basement and the mother was busy preparing a big dinner. This all seemed very natural—nobody was dead. Yet, knowing my teacher, I figured something was about to happen.

I followed her into the family room where the kids were chasing one another. They dashed wildly about until the little girl tripped on a lamp cord and caught her chin on a table edge. She received an ugly jagged gash.

No-Eyes then sped me into the kitchen. The mother had heard

the child scream out. She flinched, and the knife cut deeply into her finger.

Downstairs, unaware of the commotion above him, the father carefully guided his jigsaw over the precisely measured line. He cursed as a sliver of wood flew into his eye.

No-Eyes left the house.

"I'm glad I don't live on *this* street!" I sighed.

"Many streets gonna be like this. This no unusual street in future. This be normal future street."

We were off once again, off moving through darkness. We talked as we went. "I know what this is all about. You don't even have to explain anything."

"Good. Summer tell No-Eyes what this stuff be 'bout."

"The park, the amusement park, was to show me the accidents that will be happening in the future. The milkman showed more murders, the woman who killed her kids and then herself—that's going to be happening more too. And the old woman getting run over...."

"Wait! Summer miss stuff here."

"I did?" I thought about all that I had been shown. I didn't come up with anything else. "No I didn't."

"Think again, smart mouth."

Again I reviewed the events. Still nothing.

"Why woman take life of children and self?"

I replayed that recent conversation. "Because her husband was in jail."

"Why for?"

"For embezzlement, for stealing from his company."

"Yup. Peoples gonna need way to beat bad money stuff, remember? Peoples in big jobs gonna do bad stuff at work."

"That's called white-collar crime."

"I not care what that called! It gonna happen much. That all I know. That what No-Eyes see gonna happen. That what Summer miss in picture."

"Okay. There will be terrible amusement accidents, more murders and more suicides. Also, an increase in white-collar crime and pedestrian deaths. And accidents in the home will also increase. No-Eyes, what more could there possibly be?"

"Here, look."

We had entered a hospital. We were standing next to a nurses' station and we listened in on softly spoken words.

"They finally found out what that little Smith girl has. The tests were positive for Bubonic. That's the nineteenth one this month!"

I was really amazed this time. To think that such dreaded diseases would return in our modern times was catastrophic to say the least.

I turned to No-Eyes for comment. She was nowhere in sight. But I knew where she was. And I immediately thought of the cabin.

The familiar place was comforting. I looked about and saw her in the kitchen busily brewing up another one of her private specialties. I took the time to view my physical form. It used to be quite a shock to view one's own body separated from the mind, but I was accustomed to that now. So I hovered above my physical head and, before I descended, I saw No-Eyes nod to me.

I opened my eyes and stretched.

She brought the steaming cups into the living area and set mine down on the couch arm. She sat in her rocker. "Well?" came her whisper.

"Well that was some trip."

She shrugged. "That just way stuff gonna be, Summer." She sipped the steaming tea.

I thought it was quite incongruous, sitting there sipping tea so casually just after viewing such a gruesome future for mankind. "I don't think I want any of this," I said as I reached for the cup to return it.

"Drink up," she encouraged, "it gonna make Summer feel better."

"That's like turning away."

"Nope. That only be acceptance, that all. Summer no can change stuff anyways."

She did have a point. I sipped the mildly invigorating brew. It seemed to immediately boost my spirits. I shot her a sly look. "What's in this?"

She winked. "Summer not want to know that."

"I can guess," I teased back. "Don't forget, you've taught me formulas for just about everything, including *uppers!*"

"Shh! Summer no *say* that so loud!"

I laughed at her sudden need for secretiveness. "What's the matter? You think the police are outside listening?" I teased.

"We get to that stuff some other day. Drink up. Be still!" She furtively peered about her small room, brought her eyes to mine and smiled wide, showing a mouthful of pink gums. She was acting, but under the playful facade, she wasn't really kidding at all—she was dead serious.

Breath Heaving

*The newborn heaved great breaths
that gathered unto itself incredible
strength and power.*

My last two weekends had been utterly depressing. The burden-some heaviness of my lessons had been pressing their weight lower and lower upon my sensitive spirit. What I desperately needed was a weekend break from the Phoenix lessons. However, No-Eyes wasn't going to allow me that luxury. She wanted to complete the Phoenix material in consecutive visits. I believe that they were as difficult for her to teach as they were for me to learn. The unpleasantness of the future was hard to discuss. Yet, it would be even harder to live through when the time came.

She explained at the outset of these lessons that even though there were future dates pinpointed for each specific happening, I was not to reveal them. She cited two excellent reasons for this.

The first reason had to do with placing fear in the minds of people. This fear would be a direct result of my revealing dates and timetables of the catastrophic events. If I revealed these dates, who would then take the time to read the warning signs? These signs were to prepare the people who would be aware enough to heed them, to take the necessary positive steps for self-preservation and survival. More than once she said that in the end, after the final devastations, the Great Spirit's harvest of souls would only include those who were aware enough to listen and to heed the many signs that had been given.

The second reason had to do with the Law of Probabilities. What this boils down to, the bottom line, is that even though a specific happening shows a certain date in the future for becoming a reality, this date may fluctuate due to the direct interaction of many determining factors. In simple terms, there are many influences that can alter a foreseen date.

An example of this was when Bill's death date was altered. She said that just because his date was altered (bypassed) by my own involuntary intervention, in no way guarantees us that he will not have another. True, No-Eyes assured us that his final death date wouldn't come before a very long time, but that does not include the very viable possibility of him being directly called back by God—as so often happens.

So, it is clear that to give a specific date for *any* future event is mere folly. A knowledgeable person must never place any credence in such a prophesied date without first considering its dramatic alteration by numberless probabilities.

Now, you say, here's a bright light on a dark matter. Perhaps the catastrophic events will not even come about then. Perhaps enough factors will waylay these horrible coming events. Sorry, they *are* forthcoming. The only aspect that could possibly alter them would be the *order* of their sequence. And, it is also a possibility that *all* events foreseen by No-Eyes could end up occurring simultaneously. We must watch for the signs that are sure to come.

During the peaceful weeknights, Bill and I discussed these things. It would certainly be a confused world if the events did come about all at once. We discussed it at length and came to the conclusion that most of the events will be sequential, with some occurring simultaneously. We were both involved with making our long-term plans for our personal future.

We had taken the cue from No-Eyes and started living what she called the Earthway. We had stopped eating meat long ago, not only because of the variety of carcinogens in it but because the heaviness of the meat itself kept the physical body in such a lowered rate of vibration and, because we no longer had the desire to eat innocent animals. As a direct result, our health had greatly improved and we experienced an increase in general vitality and well-being.

I learned to mix my own herbal medicinal formulas, after being carefully taught of No-Eyes' intricate methods of meticulous preparations. And even our family's body lotions were homemade. My kitchen was brimming with glass jars of over fifty different herbs, spirits, tinctures, and oils.

We would talk long into the night about buying remote mountain property. And of course we discussed the workings of our proposed greenhouse that would be full of growing herbs and vegetables.

We never talked about large houses or material possessions. We would have little use for those in the future. The bare necessities were always first and foremost in our minds.

It was very difficult for me to relax with the everyday activities when the foreboding words of No-Eyes continued to course throughout the caverns of my mind. To me, the world was nearing the brink of its final downfall. My heart continued to remain heavy. My mind continually wandered through the terrible scenes of our psychic travels. And my spirit remained weighted. I cannot effectively convey how devastated I felt. It was hard to place my full conscious attention on the mundane aspects of daily life when it would be suddenly and unexpectedly violated by subliminal flashbacks of destruction and despair. It was hard to listen to the nightly newscasts without recognizing the beginnings of one sign, or to read the papers and find yet more signs gathering ominous momentum. And the incredible sense of urgency followed me everywhere.

I would lie in bed at night and feel a great sorrow for those who would experience the horrors-to-come. I heard their tormented cries. I felt their acute pains. And, worst of all, my skin eerily crawled when my aura sensed the icy approach of pressure from the closing in of time—it was closing in on the world like a giant vise from space. I could almost hear the creaking of its massive gears turning, turning. I would reach such a heavy point of empathy that I had to escape into the mountains to release it or I would surely go mad.

During the week, I did just that. Bill told me to get away, go for a drive. And after getting my girls off to school, I left. I got into our trusty "Betsy" and didn't even have to think about where I would go. As I drove along Highway 67, I took time to notice the brilliance of the early autumn sun that shown through the golden veins of the quaking aspens. The mountains were literally ablaze. I couldn't wait to reach my destination, for I knew I would return home a new person— emptied, yet revitalized.

I made several turns down rarely used roads. My heart pounded with anticipation. Soon I could drive no further and I walked through a wide section of jack pines, up a high hill and down through a stand of glistening aspens. And when the familiar voice of the stream beckoned to me, I knew that I was almost there. I rounded a bend and entered the sacred sanctuary that would compassionately and effectively accept my heartfelt soul song, raise it up on the wings of the wind, and place it at the feet of God.

The remainder of my week sped by and I was again faced with

another weekend with my old teacher. The days remained sunny and crisp. Some of my beautiful aspens were losing their will to stay awake. They uncaringly allowed the playful winds to whisk away their golden garments. They had shared their riches and now they laid their soul bare and nodded off to sleep until the gentle breath of spring softly blew over their shoulders again.

Yet, there remained enough autumn beauty to draw the city dwellers up to the Woodland Park and Cripple Creek areas. They came every weekend now. They'd stand by the roadsides taking pictures in every direction. I never took pictures of my favorite time of year. Pictures were flat and pale compared to the living thing. Besides, my mind continually snapped shots of my beautiful natural surroundings and it would play them back in full three-dimensional frames whenever I wished to recall them.

Late September mornings could be chillingly cold up in the mountains. Yet I drove with my window open to let the wind freely toss my hair and fill my tired being with its refreshing essence. The wind that whipped about inside my truck was filled with scents of changes. It brought visual images of joyful days of family wood gathering and pine cone hunting. It brought images of alert deer and elk herds. It brought images of Bill and I walking through silent nights of gently falling snow, and of warm dark evenings snuggled in front of the blazing fireplace. It was because of these mental images that I willingly picked up the hitchhiking autumn wind and let him ride as my passenger to No-Eyes' house that day. And it was because of his images that I felt so totally uplifted when I raced through the old woman's cabin door.

I literally flung her door back on its rusty hinges.

She was knitting in her rocker by the fireplace. "Summer blow in like winter wind!" she cackled.

I loved to see her laugh. "You like that?" I chirped. "I can do it again!" And I turned to create an instant replay of the grand entry.

"No! Summer gonna let heat out! Get *in* here!"

"Spoil sport," I playfully admonished. "Just wanted to see you laugh again." After removing my woven cape, I knelt by her chair while I raised my hands to the friendly fire that snapped and cracked.

She continued knitting as if I had actually gone back outside and stayed there. I watched the fire shadows play an energetic game of tag over her smokey log walls. There were times when silence was a priceless treasure between us. We remained in solitude for several more minutes.

Then the omen of the repeated creak and thud sent loud signals through the stillness. I turned to face her. She had set the needles down in her lap and stared ahead.

I was in a light mood. "No-Eyes," I began, "why don't we take a break this weekend and just sit around here by the fire and relax."

"That be nice, Summer," came the soft reply.

"Good, you stay where you are and I'll make us some tea." I quickly jumped up and went into the kitchen.

"But we not gonna do that," she said almost to herself.

I froze. "What? What did you say?"

She motioned for me to come and take her knitting. I did.

"We gonna keep going here. We get this future stuff all done. Then we can sit and drink tea by fire."

I was encouraged. "You mean we'll be done today?"

The old one shuffled as she pulled her chair back from the fire to the couch. And after telling me to get comfortable, she answered me. "I no say that. We gonna need maybe two more weekends yet, then we gonna be done with future stuff."

My heart sank like a lead weight. "That long?"

"It not be so long. It go by pretty fast, Summer see."

I sighed.

She gave me one of her curious knowing looks. "Summer act like she got world on shoulders."

"I did have. I had to go back up in the mountains again last week."

She dropped her head in understanding. "I sorry for that," she consoled. Then, "No-Eyes still gonna finish stuff here."

"I know. You have your job to tell me and I have my job to listen. It's really okay. I'll be all right." And I reached over to pat her knee.

She grabbed my hand. "Summer not only need to listen, Summer need tell peoples. Peoples gonna not know writing on wall when they see it. Peoples need know all signs. Peoples need know Phoenix be rising."

I rubbed her boney hand. "If you say so, I'll try."

"Summer have to try 'cause that be stuff Summer here to do. Not only 'cause No-Eyes say so."

"Yeah, I said I'd try, but I don't want to be thought of as a doomsday sayer. I told you that already."

She then patted my hand before resting back into her rocker. "Then Summer tell peoples that No-Eyes be this bad doom-sayer."

I shook my head. "That would be unfair of me. I guess we both are then."

Her shoulders shrugged. "That up to Summer."

"You're doing your part, I'll do mine."

"That all we can do, Summer. That all we here to do."

Then there was an ominous deepening silence that stealthily crept between us. I could tell there was something grave on her mind other than my present lesson. "Is something bothering you today? Do you feel okay?"

"I fine all right," she replied in a low unconvincing tone.

"No-Eyes, what is it?" I pushed.

The rocker spoke to me as I waited for the woman's reply. The creak and thud forewarned of seriousness. I waited for several heavy minutes.

"Summer," she began softly.

"Yeah?"

"There be some important stuff I got to tell you. It gonna be 'bout you. I not gonna always be 'round. I got to tell stuff 'fore it be too late."

I didn't like the sound of this. I thought she was going to talk about the day she'd be leaving the mountains—leaving me. "We already talked about your leaving. I don't want to hear anymore about that."

"Stuff not be 'bout that. Stuff be 'bout Summer."

"Me?"

She nodded sadly.

"Things about my future?"

"Nope. 'Bout past."

"Oh." I was surprised she wanted to discuss my past. She usually viewed talking of the past as a waste of the valuable energies of the present. The past was always unimportant, it was the present and the future that she considered to be most valuable.

"Summer, remember that day when No-Eyes' Indian friend tell Summer the story 'bout She-Who-Sees?"

I brightened at the memory. "Yeah! That's when I found out she was my ancestral grandmother from way back. That was certainly some day for me!"

She nervously fidgeted with the folds of her skirt. "Well, Summer . . . No-Eyes' friend not tell stuff like it really was. He not tell all stuff even. He make tiny change in story 'cause he not think Summer be ready for whole story. He mislead Summer with what he say."

This was getting interesting. "You mean he *lied* to me?"

"He not mean to do that, but it be stuff he leave out that be important here. He say She-Who-Sees be Summer's ancestral grandmother—she not be." The woman paused while the words sunk in.

They struck hard. *"What?"*

"Calm down. I gonna get stuff right here."

"I certainly hope so! If she wasn't my ancestral grandmother, then who *was* she?"

Silence permeated the cabin like a living, breathing thing.

"No-Eyes?"

She answered in a low, soft whisper. "You."

"Me!" I shouted in a sudden outburst of disbelief. "Me?"

She calmly nodded. Her wise eyes widened. "Summer, you spend last two lifes as full-blood Shoshoni. You already know 'bout life lived as Sequanu, but last life you been She-Who-Sees. Summer, remember She-Who-Sees say she see one in future who be as summer rain on hot, dry plains? That be *you*, now in *this* life. When Summer first come to woods of No-Eyes. Before No-Eyes even speak to that sad, sad woman, No-Eyes reach far back into that woman's past. No-Eyes *see* She-Who-Sees, No-Eyes *see* how she come *again* as lonely, sad woman in my woods. Most important, No-Eyes see woman's true purpose, why she been led here."

I was numb of body and mind. I couldn't find words for a few minutes, then as my mind thawed by degrees, I closed my eyes and saw the large, black eyes of She-Who-Sees, the compelling dark pools that had previously haunted my dreamscrapes, eyes that beckoned me into the swirling vortex of my present circumstances.

Yet I was exasperated at the same time. Here I was, believing this Indian woman in my past was my ancestor, and all along she was me back in my last life! I was confused and hurt all at once.

No-Eyes detected the strained air. "Summer no feel bad. Summer, peoples need to know important stuff here. *Blood* not be important here. *This*!" she beat her thin chest, "*this* be what most important! Listen now. This be important spirit lesson."

I felt the vibrations lift as she prepared to reveal a new spiritual truth—a concept I wasn't yet familiar with.

"Summer be so concern 'bout not being a *fullblood!* Blood no mean *no* stuff! Listen now. Spirit, *soul,* that what be most important."

"I know that. The soul always comes first."

"So! If soul come first, why peoples gonna care 'bout what *who* be in *blood?* Summer be fullblood Shoshoni in two lifes! That count for somethin'! Summer first been Sequanu and then been She-Who-Sees. *Now,* right now, Summer have what be called a carryover spirit. Summer have carryover Indian *soul!* That why you be *one* with forest. *That* why you *cry* so bad 'bout Indian peoples. *That* why Summer led to No-Eyes woods even! It be carryover Indian *soul* that make Summer so Indian *now!*"

This new concept was baffling. And the way she put it justified it to me. Then a fleeting thought entered my consciousness. No-Eyes perceived it before it vanished. "Go on, tell No-Eyes what you just now remembered."

"I remembered that when I first saw you, when I first came into your cabin and looked into your eyes, I saw something that I'd never seen in anyone else's eyes before. I remember thinking that it was just like looking into the eyes of She-Who-Sees, and that you said that what I was seeing...was myself. Now I understand."

The old one simply closed her eyes and nodded.

I was deeply pensive as I thought about my Indian ancestors that lived so far back in time. I was living a bizarre enigma. I understood the complex mechanics of the situation but I was unsure of my feelings about it. My teacher had asked if I understood, my only truthful reply couldn't have been anything but, "I guess."

She cocked her head. "Summer not believe No-Eyes?"

"Oh I believe you. It's just such a foreign concept, that's all."

"Many peoples today got carryover soul. It not be so new stuff here."

"Evidently not," I agreed. "But it's also not exactly common knowledge either."

"There be some other spirit truths that not be known yet also." She thought I needed further proof of this one. A barrage of questions ensued. "Where Summer live before coming here?"

"Places in Michigan; Westland, then Marquette."

"Why Summer not stay?"

"They didn't have mountains. I needed the mountains. I was too restless without them."

Her eyes danced. "Summer live in mountains for two lifes. Summer miss them. See? Summer live in *Rockies* before. See?"

Silence. But I was thinking.

She continued. "What kind of peoples Summer be interested in before?"

I thought about how I used to be obsessed with ancient Egypt and then I mentally reviewed how my interest altered. "Egyptians, East Indians, then American Indians."

"Humph. See how you work way 'round to home peoples?"

I had never thought of it in that way before. And when I analyzed my method of changing interests, how one naturally slipped into the other, I could clearly see that all along I had been subconsciously working my way around to the Native American People and culture. My searching path had led me down many trails. I had been as a lost child seeking the only thing I would identify most with—my true home.

She had more probing questions. "Why No-Eyes not ever see Summer in hard shoes?"

I questioningly frowned as I glanced down at the dusty knee-high apache boots. "Because regular shoes stifle my feet, they make my whole body feel suffocated. I hate regular shoes. Besides, in these I can feel the forest floor when I go into the woods."

"See? And tell 'bout *this!* Did Summer go to Lone Feather Council Pow Wow when it be in Woodland Park?" She was approaching a very personal and extremely touchy subject.

I slowly shook my head while I daringly stared at her.

She wisely ignored the challenge. "Why not?" she prodded further.

I would allow this to go only so far. "Well, I went into the saddle club and bought some of their beautiful handicrafts," I inched around.

"Why Summer go in there?"

Verbally creeping along, "Because I liked being around the people." God, she was just too close! I attempted to nip it in the bud. "All right, I'm Indian because of my distant ancestry *and* because of this strong carryover Indian soul. You've convinced me," I said, trying to finish off the tender subject matter.

But she would have none of it. She couldn't be stopped. And, leaning forward, peering into the depths of my soul, she needled on. "Summer go *see* Indian parade?"

"No," I whispered sheepishly.

She cleverly spread her hand next to her ear. "What? Summer *never* see Indian parade?"

I couldn't lie to her. "Only the first year."

"Humph. Why you not go see parade second year, huh Summer?"

I was quickly becoming angry with her for forcing me to talk about something that was so private—so personally humiliating. Angry war drums began thundering within my tender heart. And the hard lump of sensitivity formed deep within my constricted throat. I remained silent.

"Summer gonna have to face stuff here. Bill not even know why Summer refuse to go see second parade. What Summer do at first parade that keep her from going back next year? Huh?"

The thundering drumbeats reached their deafening crescendo. The hard lump rose to pierce the fortress around my guarded sensitivities. My tender sacred ground had been desecrated and roiling anger exploded through a torrent of welling tears. "*Stop it!* Just *stop* it! *Damn you anyway!* Okay . . . *I cried! That's* what I did! I just stood in the crowd and when I saw the Indians in their native dress the DAMNED EMPATHY rose! I burst out CRYING, No-Eyes, I CRIED just like a DAMNED BABY! THERE! Are you HAPPY now?" I dropped my head in my hands and sobbed my soul out. She had broken through my sacred ground.

My teacher rose from her rocker and sat next to me. She held me. She cradled her hurt baby. She rocked and talked softly. "That have to get out, Summer." And she held me until the tears began to ebb.

I hugged my old friend tightly. I desperately clutched onto her. I never wanted to let go.

She whispered. "Summer, we got to talk more 'bout this stuff."

I simply nodded.

"Now, why you cry like babe at that parade?"

"Because," I hedged, "because I felt so many confusing things."

The answer was unacceptable. It was too generalized. It wasn't nearly good enough. She was fishing around for the hurting' specifics that required a total release. "What confusing stuff?"

"Well, I felt hurt. I felt a terrible deep hurt that those proud Indian People were walking down mainstreet with all those white people gawking at them. And I . . .felt humiliated, deeply humiliated."

"White peoples?"

I froze. I was perplexed when the realization of my own words struck my conscious mind like a hard slap in the face. I had actually referred to the crowd of townspeople as "white!" The word had come out so naturally. "No-Eyes, I know what I just said, but that was my thought at the time."

"What *else* make Summer angry at parade?"

I immediately knew what she wanted me to admit to. And I also knew that I wasn't going to be allowed to leave this cabin until I had said it all. What I had to say embarrassed me, but she was forcing it out. "I was angered that an Indian parade would include men in Civil War uniforms. *That* angered me. I wanted to scream at them. No-Eyes, I actually *hated* the *sight* of them! I had an intense *urge* to run at them and *strike* them, claw their *eyes* out."

"'Course you did. That be natural. Summer, don't you see? The sleeping memory had stirred the carryover soul! The carryover soul memory dominated the moment!"

"Yeah, I see that now. I see how that accounts for the hatred and the sudden unexplainable urge to retaliate."

"So, why Summer cry so bad?"

Here it comes. I looked into her sightless eyes and began to feel the renewed flooding in my own begin to return. "I cried because of how beautiful Indian life used to be . . . ."

"Go on."

"I thought about how *free* they were, how they *cherished* their lands. And I thought about how everything *changed* when the *white* man came! I *cried* because they took it all *away!* They *treated* them like *animals* and *herded* us onto *barren lands!*" I caught myself and made controlled efforts to calm down before I finished with a low whisper. "And we were left with nothing but our dusty plains and the dry winds that blew our beautiful heritage away."

She squeezed my hands. "We? Us? *Our*?"

Our eyes met. "Did I say that?"

She smiled, nodded and gently brushed back my hair. "Summer," she concluded softly, "Indian *blood* not talk stuff like that. Only Indian *soul* say that stuff."

And I was convinced. "No-Eyes?"

"What?"

"What do you think people will say about this? What'll they think?"

"Humph. No-Eyes no care. Summer no care. Summer be proud. Summer have *old* Indian *soul*!" She pounded my chest proudly.

And I was proud.

For the next hour, my teacher left me in silent contemplation. I rested on the old couch and watched the firelight dance about the cozy room while the new spiritual concept of the carryover soul created its own special dance within my mind.

The concept was totally new to me and I wondered how many people like myself were living a mental culture that was so totally different from their physical one. I concluded that the past-life memory must surely be exceedingly close to the surface of the present consciousness. Mine was so close that it broke through the thin veil of time and successfully took over to dominate the present-day traits and characteristics of my personality. It was as if I were straddling the fence of time. And I wondered how many people today were living with strong past-life memories.

It was an interesting aspect of the spritual truths, an aspect that I would've never before considered. I knew a person could be regressed through hypnosis into their past lives. It was a relatively simple procedure, as I've done it for others; however, for a person to 'consciously' possess that past life memory and to have it be predominant in their present life was incredible, it could be mind-boggling. Yet, according to my wise teacher, there were many such people. They were indeed common.

I mentally retraced our conversation and I was filled with a deep regret when I came to the part where I had angrily sworn so adamantly at my dear friend. I turned to see what the old one was doing.

She had slid her rocker in front of the fire. She was staring intently into the licking flames.

I shamelessly invaded her mental privacy and found it to be full of an unfamiliar type of mixed emotions. The only word that would even remotely describe it would be a tiredness of some sort. The visionary was very old. She had previously informed me that I was to be her last student. And I knew that our time together would soon be drawing to a close. I left her alone and returned to my own thoughts.

I had come to love my old friend a great deal. She meant the world to me. I would die before hurting her in any way. She had given me the chance of a lifetime to learn from a knowledgeable spiritual teacher. And the things I learned were invaluable. She had taken a novice who thought she already was proficient in the ways and talents of the spirit, and she had brought that novice down to a basic spiritual kindergarten class before gently bringing her up through the spiritual grades to create a deep thinking and cautious graduate.

Her teaching methods would be determined by the type of lesson being taught. She could be a cupcake or a Simon Legree, but she was always successful. And I loved her deeply. I was mortified that I had lost my temper with her. I had cursed her. I couldn't rest with that unforgivable action on my conscience. I again turned to face her. "No-Eyes?" I called softly.

She remained facing the fire. "Yup?"

"I'm sorry I swore at you like that. I really am. I feel awful."

"Summer s'posed to rest now, feel good now."

I got off the couch and knelt beside her. "I can't rest—not until you know how sorry I am for what I said to you. No-Eyes, I didn't mean it, honestly. You just got me so angry. I didn't want to admit to crying like that and I knew you weren't going to give up hammering at me until I did. I'm so sorry."

"It be okay. Someday Summer gonna do some hammer stuff to help other peoples. Summer can then remember how angry she feel 'bout that. She be able to understand people's reactions better that way. No stuff wasted, even when Summer swear."

"I'm not going to badger people like that."

She looked at me. "All good teachers need to bring out peoples' hurt. They not get better without that stuff. They no can heal by holding bad hurt stuff deep inside."

"Well, I guess. But besides that, I need to hear that you forgive me."

"Summer needed to get that bad hurt stuff out."

"That's not what I want to hear."

She faced the firelight again. "No-Eyes forgive Summer. No-Eyes know it all be lesson part. Summer no make hurt here." She gently touched her chest.

I laid my head against her arm. "I never would hurt you. I never would say anything to make you feel bad, you know that, don't you No-Eyes?"

She stroked my head. "No-Eyes know."

We sat together for a long while until I felt her hand drop from my head. I lovingly peered up at her slackened face. The old one had fallen asleep and the firelight was kind to her. It softened the deep lines and bestowed a certain youthfulness to an old woman who was nearly finished with her earthly mission. I silently got up and left her to her warm peace. I curled up on the couch and protectively watched over my sleeping friend.

The quiet atmosphere of the warm room was more than mildly conducive to sleep. I found my eyelids beginning to droop. Sleep was the last thing I wanted to do now. I stood and silently did some exercises to refresh my mind. I touched my toes and swung my arms from side to side.

"Summer sound like stampeding buffalo!"

I froze in mid-bend. The sudden sound of her voice startled me. I looked up. She hadn't stirred a muscle. And I rushed to her side. "Did I wake you?"

She searched my eyes and raised one feathery brow.

"I'm sorry. I was trying to be so quiet."

She showed wide gums. "Summer be quiet 'nough. No-Eyes be woke up by thoughts. No-Eyes still have stuff to talk 'bout today."

"But I wanted you to rest. You seemed so tired."

"Tired no matter. No-Eyes got stuff to say. No-Eyes get plenty sleep some other time."

"If you're sure. How about I whip up some tea. Would you like that?"

She nodded as she straightened herself in the hard rocker.

We talked as I prepared a tea with the Siberian Ginseng and Gotu Kola that I had brought for her. "Well, what is the Phoenix doing now, during the events of this lesson?"

She raised her chest several times and let out great long breaths. "He be breathing heavy, Summer. He be taking in big breaths of air. This air bring much strength to his being. Breaths send energy and power through his body. He gonna store energy for his grand take-off. He gonna then fly low over all land. But now he just be getting ready. He be heaving breath."

"I see," I said, bringing the tea into her. "Are you too warm by the fire? We could move back a bit."

"I fine. Sit down, Summer."

I sat next to her chair, then remembering that she had sternly admonished me about sitting with my legs crossed, I reclined on my side.

"This not be long lesson here, not like next weekend, but it still be important stuff even."

"It's *all* important. It's all going to be relevant—to add to the total scope of warning signs. No-Eyes, every single sign, no matter how insignificant it may appear, will serve to alert people of the ultimate end that it precedes."

"Summer say that stuff better than No-Eyes."

I smiled. "Who did the teaching?"

"I not teach Summer to write. Summer have own way of writing 'bout what in heart. Summer put heart on paper."

"I'll just tell it like it is, No-Eyes."

The old woman stared thoughtfully into the flames. "Summer tell 'bout Phoenix days?"

"I said I would, didn't I?"

"Yup. Summer write stuff down, peoples read, peoples decide in heart what be true here. Some peoples gonna believe stuff. Some peoples gonna no believe. Then they gonna watch, listen for signs to come. Even peoples who no believe stuff gonna watch anyways—they not sure they no believe."

"I suppose."

The rocker began its prelude. "We get going on stuff now." She glanced at the window. "It be late," Creak-thud. "Summer, few days ago, we talk 'bout how monies stuff gonna change. We talk much 'bout bad times coming for peoples money."

"I remember."

"That gonna go on all over, not only here, but it gonna be in other countries even. Monies gonna be bad between countries. They gonna have no monies for each other, Summer see?" She gave me the go ahead to reword her meaning. "Summer put right words to that stuff."

"I'll try, as long as I understand what you're saying. Let's see," I paused to recap our former discussion, "America will have a large scale economic depression, farmers won't be able to get loans—nobody will, banks and the stock market will fail, industries will shut down and there'll be a sharp decline in property values. Now you're saying that these things will be worldwide, right?"

"Yup."

"And there will be no money borrowed or loaned between countries."

She nodded.

"Then you're saying that this economic depression will not only adversely affect the private sector, but it will also be widespread in the government treasuries too."

"That right."

"Then I assume the governments will be in massive debts to each other, with none being able to recoup their income from the people's

76

taxes or from industrial revenues or from foreign import taxes."

"That what No-Eyes say. Yup, that how it gonna be."

I thought on that one. This would certainly have devastating consequences. "But you said that the government would help the unemployed through increased taxation of the people. How can that be if the government now has no money coming in?"

"This be later in time, Summer. Remember?"

"Okay, first the people will be heavily taxed to pay for the welfare assistance programs, and then they won't be" I shook my head. "There's something missing here. What's going to stop the taxation so dramatically?"

"That stuff be for next lesson. Summer got stuff right for now."

"Just don't forget to fill in the gaps," I cautioned.

"No-Eyes not forget. We gonna get to gaps later." She sipped her tea. "Now, countries gonna be angry at each other. They gonna be in much bad shape. Peoples gonna be hurting bad. Countries gonna look 'round for somebody to put blame on. They gonna want to fight. They gonna take monies they got and make war stuff, see?"

"Hold on a minute. Let's look at what we've got so far. The leaders of the different countries will attempt to blame the other leaders for their problems. Then, in an effort to shift the blame, they'll build up their arsenals. No-Eyes, countries already have more than they need to blow this whole planet away right now. Why would they waste what was left of their money on that?" I was disgusted. "This is not at all logical."

She clucked her tongue. "*No* war be logical. But this move, this war move by many countries gonna be only threat stuff. It be way to show peoples how they can be strong, how they can protect."

"That's ridiculous." I was sick of the insane arms race. "No-Eyes, people just *have* to have more say in what their country does."

"That coming next week. That be in lesson next week. But Summer be right 'bout weapon race being silly. Too bad leaders not see stuff like No-Eyes see. Too bad they not see past big heads. They not see how they gonna do all that war stuff for nothing."

Silence.

"New countries gonna make nuclear bombs too even," she cleverly slipped in.

"*New* countries?"

"Little ones."

We had a communication problem here. I named a few small countries but she wasn't familiar with them and she didn't know the right names either. But she did say that they looked different from Americans.

I began a separate line of questioning. "Are these people light-skinned?"

"Nope."

"Yellow?"

"Humph! They got nuclear stuff long time! Where Summer been? They got much stuff under Earth Mother."

I ignored this new information and continued with my line of questioning. "Then are they brown?"

"Yup. They be brown."

This narrowed it down somewhat but, because she still didn't know the name of the countries, I was unable to pinpoint them. "I guess that'll have to due for now. So, various countries will be placing their economic troubles on other countries causing them to gear up for war. Now, my next question is, will they actually go through with war?"

Creak-thud.

"No-Eyes?"

The rocker stopped. "Tiny stuff."

"Tiny? You call *any* war *tiny* stuff?"

She spoke calmly. "I not gonna go on here if Summer gonna get so upset."

"Well you can hardly blame me. I mean, after all, a war is a war. *No* war is tiny, No-Eyes. If just *one* life is lost then it's *not* tiny."

"No-Eyes say tiny 'cause they not gonna be big bomb stuff. They no gonna send big bombs."

"*They*? You mean there'll be *more* than *one* tiny war?"

"Yup. No-Eyes just say that many countries gonna blame many other countries. Summer not listen good."

"Well hell! You're not speaking too good. You're making me read between your words. This is important, No-Eyes!"

"That what No-Eyes say before. No-Eyes say this stuff be important here. Besides, Summer no swear."

I relaxed. "I won't swear if you won't leave things out."

"I not leave no stuff out here. No-Eyes teach Summer to listen good. No-Eyes expect that here too even."

I respectfully reconsidered. "You're right. I apologize. My mind was miles ahead when you began talking about the arms escalation. I just assumed it would be between America and Russia."

She clucked her tongue again. "Summer not ever assume *no* stuff—*ever!*"

I was embarrassed that I had become so inexcusably lax in my thinking, especially so boldly in front of my teacher. "I'm sorry."

"Summer be no good when mind come to ideas and conclusions that not be there in first place."

I stared down into my cup. "I usually don't. It's different between us. I mean, whenever we talk together like this, well, it's a very personal interaction and we usually know what's on the other's mind. I've come to understand your meanings without much being actually verbalized."

"That be true, Summer. But that no mean Summer not listen good anymore."

I stood rightly corrected. I was still a learning student.

"Now, No-Eyes say wars be tiny 'cause many, many of them gonna go on all over. They gonna have American boys in many, many different lands. They gonna be fighting all over, see?"

"In Russia?"

"Nope. They fight in little countries, many different little countries."

"But no nuclear missiles, right?"

"That right."

Silence.

"That good, huh Summer? That good no nuclear stuff then?"

Silence.

"Summer?' She crouched forward to peer at me.

"*No* war is good. I'm so sick of wars and fighting and discord. I wish it would all end. I wish the end was here right now. I wish the Phoenix was flying free."

"He be soon, Summer. He be soon 'nough."

Wings Flexing

*And the fledgling craned his
downy neck as he unfolded and
flexed the mighty wings of change.*

Sunday morning brought me a most enjoyable surprise. Autumn had again thoughtfully laid down a wonderful warm blanket over the day. It appeared that perhaps Indian Summer was going to stay with us for a while. My drive was filled with warm air circulating through the cab of the truck. I breathed deeply. I longed to hold onto the scent of this Indian Summer, for it would soon be gone, whisked away just as suddenly as it had come.

As I drove along the twisting mountain roads, I thought of many things. I thought about the wars that were to come. Then a curious notion shot through my ponderings. I wondered if a new man in the White House would have a positive effect upon the probabilities of the wars-to-come. Perhaps No-Eyes foresaw the wars if the White House resident remained unchanged. But here was a very viable change factor with the future international policies and actions of a new President. Perhaps the strong probability of the wars could be bypassed after all.

I pulled the truck over and left it at the end of the road. It was a fantastic mountain morning and I was now concerned if I could successfully coax my old friend from the cabin. Such glorious days were not created for people to spend within the confinement of walls.

No-Eyes was inside. She was busy stacking up her woodpile

against the stone fireplace.

"You won't be needing that today," I informed cheerfully.

Grumble. Grumble. "Maybe I no can see with eyes, but No-Eyes can still *feel*! Summer think No-Eyes lose marbles? This stuff for other day."

"Don't have to bite my head off."

"Summer no have to think No-Eyes be stupid either."

I helped her finish stacking the wood. "It's gorgeous out this morning. It's real warm and the...."

"No-Eyes been outside to greet day already. Summer do that? Huh?"

"Not since school started again. You know I have to get the girls off and then I have to...."

"Today no school. Today be Sunday," came the reply.

"Well...." She had me right were she wanted me and I knew it.

"Well? What excuse Summer gonna try this time?"

Silence.

A low monotone broke the stillness. She poked my stomach with her boney finger. "Summer not greet day 'cause she and Bill always be filling bellies!"

She was right. Every morning we went out for breakfast at a little restaurant in Woodland. But I wasn't going to let her take that daily enjoyment away from me. "So? We enjoy that. We don't get out that often. Besides, after living together for nineteen years we deserve to get out and...."

"I not say Summer and Bill no deserve. Stop defending stuff. No-Eyes not say it not be okay."

I hesitated. "You certainly sounded like it wasn't."

She shrugged. "Summer feeling guilty maybe?"

"Of course not!"

The grin widened. "Summer certainly sound like it."

Impasse.

"Aren't we circling again, No-Eyes?"

"Yup. We go 'round, 'round and 'round sometimes. That okay. That way we play."

"I do love you." And I hugged her tightly while attempting a suggestion. "As long as you're in such a playful mood today, how about moving the classroom outside."

She pulled back and mentally studied me at arms length.

"Well? Can we?"

"Summer go fix up chairs. No-Eyes be right out."

I was so excited I nearly tripped over myself in the rush to get out. I heard the old one click her tongue and mumble under her breath. I didn't care how over-emotional she thought I was, I was too filled with elation. I arranged the chairs in the sun and pulled up the rickety pine table between them. And after surveying my work I hurried back into the cabin.

"That be fast," she said.

"I'm not done. Hurry out," I shouted back at her after grabbing two flat pillows from the couch and rushing back outside to place them on her chair.

"Summer gonna move all cabin outside?" she cackled as she carefully descended the steps.

"Just wanted you to be comfortable."

"That nice," she commented sitting down, "but we not gonna get too comfortable here. No-Eyes gonna first see if Summer gonna get lessons in head or mountains in head."

I breathed in the heady autumn air and leaned back to face the early sun. "I'll listen real good. I promise."

She doubtfully shook her head. "Summer look like she ready to bring up spirit wings."

I sharply pulled myself back to attention.

"That better."

I sighed, then breathed heavy again. "No-Eyes! Just *smell* the *air!*"

The old one suddenly made frantic movements to go back inside. She mumbled and groaned. "We *gonna* go back *in!*"

"No! I'll be good. I was just teasing."

The single brow raised again.

"Really, I was only playing."

She leaned back as if to give me another chance, as if she were testing me.

I stopped my kidding and turned my attention to the serious lesson that was forthcoming. I was here to learn from her and I always needed to outwardly express that I was inwardly prepared to learn. However, this remained a great conscious effort whenever the lessons were conducted outside. If I expected to remain here I had to expend additional energy on my mental alertness instead of my mental wanderings. So I straightened up and wriggled around in the hard chair until I was reasonably comfortable.

"Summer squirm like worm in bird mouth."

"I don't have pillows like somebody else I know."

"Humph." She listened for me to reach a satisfactory stage of comfort. When the sounds of my squeaking chair stopped, she spoke. "Summer comfortable now?"

"Not really, but it won't get any better, so shoot."

As usual, she hesitated before speaking. It was something she had admonished me to do whenever I was in a discussion with anyone. She said that it kept wrong words from coming out, it gave the mind additional thought time. "Summer, Phoenix be fledgling now. He got bigger feathers. He got much power, strength. He gonna reach neck up high and shake wings. Phoenix gonna spread wings out wide." She folded her arms in and made flapping movements before throwing them out far in the air.

"What will this represent?"

"Many stuff. He spreading, trying wings. That mean he be ready for break away time. He get ready to test himself. Peoples gonna do stuff like that too. Peoples gonna get ready to be free, free in mind."

I frowned. "I don't think I get the connection. Well, I do see the relationship, but I don't understand exactly what the people are doing. How are they mentally breaking free?"

"Peoples gonna *do* that some other time. Now they just getting *ready* for that stuff. Now stuff gonna happen that make peoples *want* to be free of stuff. See?"

"I think so. Events are going to happen that will make people uneasy, mentally. These happenings are going to test people and begin a questioning process that will increase in time. Is that sort of what you mean?"

She nodded. "That what No-Eyes say."

"What kind of events are we talking about now?"

"Many different stuff. We gonna go one stuff at time. Summer need get this right. This be important."

"All right, but are we taking them in order?"

"Order? There no order here. All stuff gonna come when time be right." She spread her fingers. "Too many different stuff here. To many free wills here to make final order."

"Then some of the happenings hinge directly on free will decisions, on too many uncertain probabilities."

She agreed.

"Is there any probability that could occur that would totally eliminate any of the events?"

"Nope. They all gonna happen. They gonna all come 'bout. There just not be firm order, that all."

"That makes things hard for people to spot. They require some time sequence. Can you foresee any of these events happening simultaneously?"

"Maybe. Maybe not. That too hard to tell here. That can be, but it still gonna depend on probability stuff. I no can give Summer order today."

"That's all right. As long as I get the events straight that'll be good enough. People can still recognize something if it's concrete enough. I guess the specific order doesn't really matter as long as the signs are clear and recognizable."

"Yup, that all peoples gonna need."

It was such a beautiful day that it took a concentrated effort for me to force my unwilling mind to accept the bad news that was forthcoming. I squirmed in the chair and awaited the old woman's revelation of the first event.

"No-Eyes gonna maybe need word help here, Summer," she began.

"We usually figure it out. Go ahead."

"Stuff in peoples world be much in order now, great order from many years ago. Stuff that no change over many, many years."

"The word is 'established.' It means something that has been set up and run the same way for years and years. Does that sound like what we want here?"

Eyes squinted under furrowed brows. "What that word again?"

"Established."

She thought. "Yup. No-Eyes talk 'bout this establish laws of countries and spirit beliefs. They gonna...."

"Wait a minute. Let's say government and religion."

After a quick mental check, she accepted that as being correct. "We got established government and religion now. This religion be here long, long time. It have one big leader."

That was simple. "The Catholic religion has one leader. He's called the Pope."

"Yup, it gonna be that one. This leader gonna die. He not gonna die 'cause he be sick. Somebody gonna kill him. Maybe everybody not know how he die. It look like maybe they gonna cover it up, push fact under rug. No matter, he gonna be killed anyways."

Silence.

"That not be new stuff, Summer. That no new stuff. After he gone, the new leader gonna make new belief laws. They gonna be in government stuff even."

"But there's a separation between religious people and the government people. This isn't right what you're saying. This is called the separation of Church and State and it's been around for a very long time."

"Nope. That maybe what it called now, but it gonna change. Church leader gonna get many hands in state laws. They not gonna be happy with stuff. They gonna get into law stuff and big trouble gonna come."

"So, the Church will become more involved with the government.

The Church will interfere?"

"Yup."

"It'll interfere with the government after the death of the Pope and the government won't like it." I thought more. "You said there'd be a lot of trouble over this. Will the government retaliate?"

"What that?"

"Get back."

"Yup."

"The government will begin interfering with the Church."

She nodded in agreement.

"The government will be able to dictate, tell the Church what to do?"

"That way it gonna be. It gonna put many hands in many churches even."

I boldly stated a fact. "No-Eyes, the government has never had any claims or rights to dictate Church laws or proceedings. There has always been a definite line of separation there."

"I no care. No-Eyes tell what seen here! Church gonna talk out loud 'bout bad state (government) laws. State gonna get back. It gonna get to Church leaders through more Church laws. They gonna fight."

"Not literally."

"No bodies, only put fingers in other's stuff. Make bad trouble."

I told her about how the Church had opened up in recent years regarding its taking a firm stand on certain political issues that it didn't agree with. I explained to her about the abortion controversy and how the Church spoke out against it. And she agreed that the writing was already visible on the wall.

"Summer, this stuff between state and Church gonna make many peoples angry. Peoples gonna be much angry and they gonna no like Church. Some gonna no like state. State gonna no like peoples. It be bad stuff for all."

"I can see the implications."

"There be more here. Peoples gonna question stuff. They not be happy with answers."

I kept trying to make clarifying statements. "Questions about the Church and state disagreements and intrusions."

"That only begin stuff. That begin peoples questions. Peoples gonna see stuff they no believe before."

The issue had become cloudy. "It's time to slow down. The Church and state event will make people question. But what will the people see that will make them question further? And question who, Church or state?"

"Both! Peoples gonna see new beings. Beings gonna come more, much more. They come from there." She pointed to the sky.

"You mean the alien beings, the U.F.O.'s."

Remaining serious, she simply nodded. "Beings gonna show more and more. They no gonna hide, play games. It be time they show they be really here all 'long."

I was visibly relieved about this news. "No-Eyes, that's wonderful! People need to see them so they can put the rumors to rest once and for all!"

"Humph."

"What's the matter? Don't you agree that it would be a good thing?"

"Maybe. Maybe not. It be good when peoples believe 'cause they gonna see with own eyes. They gonna have to believe. It not be good when peoples gonna question state 'bout stuff state already know 'bout for long time. They gonna be plenty angry at state. They gonna want to know why state hide stuff from people. This gonna make people no trust state."

"Still. . .it's better to finally have it all out in the open."

"I not done here. Peoples gonna question *Church* now. How 'bout what Church say 'bout spirits? How 'bout what Church say 'bout first man, first woman? Summer, that no stand up now! Peoples gonna be much angry at Church too even."

"It's still a wonderful thing. No-Eyes, don't you see? The only thing left for people to believe in will be the bare truth of the matter. So the Church teachings weren't quite accurate, and the government made a coverup; that just leaves the truth! Well, I think it's well past time for it."

She shrugged. "Summer have to live through it. Maybe Summer change mind later."

"Nope," I insisted. "I'll be looking forward to this one with great anticipation! I can't wait to see the skeptics with their jaws hanging open."

A balled fist struck the chair arm. "That no *way* for Summer to act!"

"Maybe. Maybe not," I grinned contentedly.

"Summer be bad student here."

"Nobody's perfect," I said mischievously.

"Summer have smart *mouth*!"

"No I don't. You told me that I wouldn't be here if I was perfect."

"Now Summer twist No-Eyes' words back like rattlesnake!"

I leaned forward. "No-Eyes, come on, you know I'm just playing with you. Don't you think I have a right to see people be shocked to discover that there really are aliens in the U.F.O.s? Especially some of the same people who humiliated me and thought I was crazy?"

She softened. "Maybe so."

"No-Eyes, I have a right to feel a certain justice done when I'm finally proven out."

She threw her hands up. "Summer be right. Summer do have that right."

We paused in our lesson while I took the time to make us lunch. I left my teacher in the shade while I made us some chicory coffee and mixed an assortment of nuts and seeds that I had brought with me. As I busied myself about her kitchen I had a satisfied smile on my face, at least until a new thought stabbed through my mind. I perked up and rushed our lunch out to the table.

"Summer gonna spill stuff! Ants gonna eat No-Eyes' lunch!"

"I just had this great idea! What if people begin questioning *other* things, *real* spiritual things—concepts? I mean, seeing and then believing in the aliens will shoot their former beliefs to kingdom come! They'll naturally begin searching farther. One thing will lead to the next and, before you know it, they'll . . . ."

She was beaming.

My ranting abruptly stopped short. "You knew all along I'd come to that conclusion, didn't you!"

The sneaky little woman purposely avoided my eyes and looked around into the trees. I felt somewhat deflated when I realized that my sudden brainstorm was expected. "Well, even if you knew it, I think this is a great lesson. Just *think* of all the things that will naturally follow!"

She turned and reached for her cup. "Summer be most funny student No-Eyes ever have," she chided.

"That's all right, go ahead and have a good laugh. But I'm really enjoying this." I scooped up a handful of sunflower seeds, raisins, almond slivers, and yogurt chips, popped them into my mouth and set the bowl on my teacher's lap. "I can't wait to tell Bill about this. He's gonna love it!"

No-Eyes efficiently munched with hard gums as she shook her head over my increasing excitement.

New realizations were coming to me faster than I could get them verbalized. I began ranting again until she put a stop to her student's babbling. "Summer gonna be teacher here?"

Sudden silence.

The old one finished chewing and sipped some of the black coffee.

I waited.

Then she picked at the seed mixture one at a time and slowly ate in silence. She drank and ate as if she were alone, as if there was no over-anxious person sitting across from her. And if I hadn't known her better, I'd have sworn that the old one had forgotten I was there at all. But I did know her. She *didn't* have a sudden case of amnesia. I did know that this frigid shoulder was one of her clever methods of cooling a student down. She'd ignore him completely until the student had reached an acceptable level of inner calm. She was going to have to ignore me for a long time today because I was literally trembling with excitement. This one had been good news of wonderful changes instead of the painful ones of devastation and death.

I rested my head back on the chair and stared up into the thick blue sky. Small tufts of white stretched out long in the high air. I could clearly imagine some great invisible baker pulling and tugging on the creamy clouds of taffy. I watched in tranquil fascination as one section in particular lengthened so far that a wide hole developed within its center; yes, it was just as if God was up there pulling on vanilla taffy.

I sighed. The mountain chickadees were beginning to riot in the nearby firs, their noisome gossiping sent out a high-pitched language throughout the forest. And the stream that sparkled in the valley's sunlight sent up ripples of background music to the soothing melody of the windsong that continually lilted through the pines.

I closed my eyes. The symphony of the spheres beckoned to my opened spirit. I let it in.

"Summer stay *here!*"

The music carried me into itself. I thought I heard a remote muffled voice, a weak faraway voice. I drifted onward, upward.

"*Summer!*"

A note of disagreeable discord rent the fine fabric of my journey. My body shuddered. My eyes flew open.

The old one smiled wryly as she leaned back smuggly into her chair. "Where Summer think she going?"

I had been mentally unnerved by her rude vocal jerk. She had caused a mild shockwave through my sensitive psyche. Her waiting ruse had indeed succeeded, because I was calmed enough to completely relax and journey off through one of nature's many multidimensional portals. In fact, I had actually begun my distant journey when I was so shockingly interrupted. "You wanted me to settle down and that's exactly what I did."

"I not say Summer can go *off* somewheres. I not say it okay to *leave* No-Eyes!"

She was a clever one she was. She knew exactly *what* I had been doing and *when* I had been doing it. She let me get completely out and on my merry way before shouting at me. So I played at her own game and gave her a taste of her own bitters. "That's very peculiar," I said with a confused look of amazement on my face, "I could've sworn that you didn't even know I was here!"

Her brows darted down to meet in a frowning whispy vee. "No-Eyes think she hear a smart mouth 'round here." She animated her sarcasm by cocking her head and spreading a leathery hand behind her ear.

I checkmated by following suit. I cocked my own head to listen. I turned to look around to my right, my left, behind me. "That's strange," I whispered mysteriously, "*I* don't hear anything."

The woman vigorously shook her head in disbelief. "I *no* time *ever* get student like Summer! I *no* have smart mouth student, ever!"

Ignoring the outburst, I kept it up by continuing to look around for this bad incorrigible student with the disrespectful smart mouth.

"Summer!"

"What!" I snapped back in feigned surprise.

She glared hard at me. Her onyx pools bored angrily into my mahogany doe-eyes that blinked innocently back at her.

Burning glowering.

Wide-eyed blinking.

Lips curling up.

Grinning.

The impasse was broken by the joyous cackle of released laughter along with the crack of a slapped knee. "Summer be *some* student. No-Eyes not ever have student who can charm snake like Summer can. No-Eyes not ever have student who *play* with No-Eyes like Summer do."

My innocent countenance melted into a wide grin. "I can't help it. I love you. I love to play with you and tease around together. When I make you angry, I fix it—I make you laugh."

"No-Eyes get many, many peoples comin' here. No-Eyes not ever got one that be so full with easy sunshine like Summer be." Then she paused before saying, "it be true. Summer be like rain on dry hot plain all right."

I became thoroughly pleased with myself when we shared playful times such as this. I was pleased to be able to bring a little gaiety into my old friend's serious life. I was glad in my heart that I could make her laugh. Even though my occasional slip into sin, my swearing, upset her, I could still manage to turn that too around into a humorous situation. She thought my easy humor was unique, it wasn't, it had been a lifelong crutch for coping with seemingly unbeatable odds. I'm sure she understood that, however, she found it a refreshing method of bluffing around the bad hands that life so often dealt me.

"We gonna go on now," she informed finishing her coffee.

"Okay." And I too matched my mood with that of the altered

tone.

"Summer think this lesson stuff here be such great one. No-Eyes think that too, but just 'cause peoples gonna question Church stuff, state stuff, it not mean they gonna come up with right answers, see?"

I didn't. "What'll be left but the truth?"

Her thin arms spread wide. "Truth be here all time! Truth no hide behind the cottonwood tree. It not sleep under that big rock. It no hide in some dark cave. Summer, truth be here all 'long. Peoples no see it before, they no see it now even."

I didn't like her insinuation. "I hear what you're saying, what your intent is, but I don't think I comprehend it. I'm not saying that I don't believe you either, but if people actually see aliens, then why in God's name wouldn't that naturally lead them to the truth of the matter?"

She upturned one palm, then the other. "Some gonna find truth. Some no find truth. It gonna be just like all time before. Summer, peoples always gonna come up with *excuse* to no believe stuff."

"But that's just plain ignorance! Why, by then it'll be right in front of their noses!"

"It be there all 'long anyways. Do peoples see it, believe it now when it already here?"

"No because they'll need more proof, more substantial proof. The aliens will *be* that living proof."

"Now we come to other stuff here. Peoples always have proof before too. Listen Summer, this be important. Proof be one thing, but there be more that peoples gonna need to have. If peoples always have proof of truth that be always in front of noses, why peoples no believe then. Huh?"

I didn't know, and I told her so. People frustrated me with their constant narrow-minded demands for proof of this and show me that. When all they had to do all along was to simply look within themselves. Nobody wanted to expend the initial effort to do so. "I don't know why they don't believe the evidence."

"Summer sure?"

I shook my head. "They just can't accept any kind of foreign concept."

She nodded disgustedly.

Silence. Then I realized what I had said. "Acceptance? That's it, isn't it. They merely refuse to accept! But why?"

She shrugged. "Peoples make own reasons. Many reasons be 'cause they no want to accept that they be wrong all 'long. Many reasons be 'cause they no want to accept that they not be best, most smart beings. Many reasons be 'cause they no want. . . . "

"Want. Want. Don't want this, don't want that! No-Eyes, there's no *wanting anything* here! It's as black and white, it's as cut and dried as it'll ever get! Yet you're saying that because of people's wants, their overblown egos, they're going to *deny* the solid proof?"

"Yup."

This was incredulous. And now I was the one who didn't want to accept peoples non-acceptance. I pouted.

"Summer no take stuff so hard. There still be many, many peoples who gonna accept proof. They gonna hold it like it be some great piece of gold even."

I brightened. "Well you made it sound like nearly everyone was going to reject it."

"Nope. I no make stuff sound like that. Summer assume stuff again."

"Well, even if I did, I'm glad that there'll be *some* people who will see the light."

"Many, many peoples gonna wake up here. They gonna grab golden truth. They gonna hold it and change lifes even. Many peoples gonna change and be new, different. Aliens gonna talk, touch, teach even. Aliens gonna prove stuff. They gonna try to help peoples here."

I wiped away the mist that had formed over my eyes. "No-Eyes, that day should've come long ago. People are so far behind. They've been thinking in the Dark Ages. It appears to me that it'll still be too late for realizations by the time the Phoenix has developed this far along."

"It never be too late for truth. Truth be light in dark Phoenix days."

"Truth is the light on *any* day. What I'm getting at is, it'll be too late for those newly aware people to make preparations."

She tilted her head to peer at me. "Too late for what, Summer?"

"For their survival," I snapped back.

Eyes narrowed. "Survival of what, Summer? What they gonna need to save?"

"Themselves!"

She hesitated as she craned forward and stared calmly into my flaring eyes. She spoke with slow deliberation. "Bodies? Or spirits?"

Silence.

The medicine woman rested her elbows on her knees. "See? It already gonna be too late for peoples to save bodies. What be most important here, Summer? Summer be missing point. Spirit be most important. Peoples who believe after they accept gonna be okay. See?"

I did. "Yeah, but they won't. . . ."

"They not gonna be in safe place with own food growing. They not gonna have survive stuff stored away 'cause they not ever believe 'nough to read signs 'bout when stuff comin'. They not be aware 'nough. They not listen without proof 'cause they not want to be put out. They love possessions stuff too much. That be like many peoples Summer cry 'bout now. But many peoples gonna be okay, Summer. They not gonna have time to save body, they gonna wake up in time to save spirit. That big advance for peoples' spirit. That be what life 'bout anyways, see?"

I saw, but that didn't make it hurt any less. "Yeah, you're right. I still feel bad about their physical though." I paused to glance into the deep forest. The smokey rays of sunlight speared through the trees and flooded the floor. It reminded me of a fantasyland—the reality that Maxfield Parrish painted from. "I'm glad they'll be advancing their souls though."

"Good! Now . . . there be many, many peoples that gonna believe, they gonna believe in spirit gifts too." She let this sink into my melancholy mind.

"Will the paranormal be generally accepted then?"

"Most peoples will."

"But not as proven fact," I added dejectedly.

She slapped her knee. "Yup, *fact!* But there still be peoples who no accept, remember?"

She snatched away my own ray of hope just as quickly as she had given it. "I guess there'll always be skeptics," I sighed.

"Yup, always gonna be."

"But I don't understand that, the skeptics I mean. No-Eyes, the abilities of the spirit are so beautiful! And they've always seemed so natural to me. I realize they're nothing that can be voluntarily turned on and off like a light switch, but when they're operating, they seem no different than seeing or hearing or touching or breathing. And why are these things considered *extra* senses? That always frustrated me, really angered me."

"Summer no try to change peoples."

"I'm not inclined to change anyone." Then I realized she was right. I possessed a deep and passionate hatred for the unaware reasoning of skeptical people. I didn't actually hate the people per se, I hated their ignorant disbelief. I believed in the paranormal because its workings came so natural to me. I had always lived with the proof of the thing. It was an undeniable fact—a part of my life. Yet, whenever I came across a skeptic, I boiled inside. I boiled at their "intellectual logic" for debunking it. And I became angry at the U.F.O. skeptics as well. Yet, when you've personally witnessed eight or nine of the flying vehicles, some seen reasonably close, you don't argue with the confirmed skeptic—you don't even bother to open your mouth. "No, I won't try to change people, No-Eyes."

"Many peoples gonna change without Summer. They gonna

change all alone. They gonna see, believe, change."

I attempted to continue where we had left off before I mentally became upset with the skeptics. "If many people will believe in the truth, the spiritual gifts, then will there also be a generalized *mass* awareness of these gifts in the future?"

Her sightless eyes brightened. "Yup. It gonna be big move to learn. They gonna seek all information, all books 'bout stuff. It gonna be big move to peoples' awareness."

"That's good, No-Eyes. Even though I can't help feeling that it'll be sort of after the fact, it'll still be a good thing. The more people who become aware of how things really are, the more spirits will be advanced. I'm glad of that. That's the real bottom line I guess."

"Yup. Summer no forget 'bout spirit life even. Peoples gonna search in books, in teachers, in hearts. They gonna find spirit truth 'bout after physical death. Peoples gonna believe more in spirit life stuff even."

This didn't surprise me. "Wouldn't that come naturally? If they believe in the gifts of the spirit, they'd automatically see how it lives on after bodily death."

The woman's shoulders slumped with the deep solemn sigh. "Nope. Listen, Summer. Some peoples gonna be only *part* aware. They gonna think *all* spirit gifts be *mind* part. They think gifts be in mind, not be spirit stuff."

Oh God. "You mean they'll believe that it's *only* a *physical* sense?"

She nodded sorrowfully.

"And that there's no *spirit* involved at *all?*"

"Yup."

This wasn't turning out to be the wonderful lesson I had initially anticipated.

"Summer, there still be peoples who no believe in Great Spirit. They think gifts be part of mind work." She shrugged. "That okay, Summer no worry 'bout those peoples. There be many, many peoples who gonna believe in spirit life stuff. They gonna be ready to die, they know truth in hearts."

"Then tell me this. Does it look like the *afterlife* of the spirit will be generally accepted?"

"It look like it."

Her answer was somewhat of a relief although not a great one. "Why does the existence of the spirit remain to be such an ongoing controversy? I can't fathom the scope of disbelief when there has been so much proof. Even when people have been placed under the deep trance of hypnosis and have regressed into past lives, the skeptics still continue to reach down into their ragged bag of logic to dig out an excuse to disbelieve. It blows me away."

She was sympathetically understanding. "We come full circle, Summer. We get back to acceptance here. They not gonna accept stuff they no want to believe in. They got many reasons to no accept. They find stuff too hard to accept, that all."

And I too found stuff too hard to accept. But I had accepted the natural aspects of life since I was very young. Now that I was older, wiser, I had to learn to accept non-acceptance. It wasn't easy.

The Wailing

The fledgling spoke.
Its chilling wail echoed an eerie
omen over all the land.

Once again I had been given another week to digest the new material. Bill and I spent many nights talking long into the early morning hours. He too was at first mislead into thinking that my last lesson was one that gave reason to rejoice. He had made the identical error of assumption that I initially had. When I thoroughly explained the total picture, he was less enthusiastic about the new awareness of the truth that was coming to the people. He too felt that it would be after the fact, too late. Yet we both knew that it was never too late for a spirit's awakening, even if it came at the last moment of physical life.

During this particular week, several of our family dinner conversations revolved around the spiritual truths. These impromptu discussions were usually initiated by a thought-provoking question by one of our girls. They had grown up knowing about the natural gifts of the spirit and every aspect that the truths encompassed. And, considering the enormous scope of concepts the truth covered, their active minds developed highly intelligent questions. These special dinners frequently lasted quite a long time. We'd sit for hours with emptied plates before us, talking candidly as one question naturally led to others. These times were most enjoyable for us all.

One day during this week, my youngest daughter, Sarah, began doing all types of extra chores for me. She noticed that I appeared particularly tired as I rested in the Boston Rocker. And entering the living room, she came up beside me. "Can I brush your hair, mom?"

I nearly fell off the chair. "Why? I thought you were going out to ride horses with Carrie?"

She sheepishly pulled a hairbrush out from behind her back. "I just thought it'd make you feel better if I brushed your hair."

Something was up. A mother doesn't need to be psychic to detect some things. It was a beautifully sunny day, the girls were off from school and were anxious to be about their playtime. Something was definitely up. "Sarah, you've been doing things for me all morning, now tell me why you don't want to go out to play."

She studied her tennis shoes. "I do wanna go out."

"Then go ahead. I'm all right," I reassured, patting her backside to send her off.

She remained beside the chair. "But can I brush it just for a little while?"

I pulled her over to me and sat her on my lap. I was going to get to the bottom of this thing yet. "Tell you what, we'll make a deal. I'll let you brush my hair if you tell me why you want to."

Her small fingers played with the bristles. "You won't laugh at me?"

I frowned. "Have I ever?"

She shook her long cornsilk hair.

"Then?"

"Well . . . I want to make sure my record shows more good things than bad things."

I smiled at her touching thought. "Are you worried that your spirit record won't balance out?"

She nodded.

"Sarah, I'm sure it looks just fine, but if you think you'd like to add a few more good deeds to it, that's fine with me."

She smiled wide, jumped off and brushed her tired mom's hair.

After I sent her outside, Bill and I talked about the incident. We were well satisfied with our children's deep comprehension of the difficult spiritual concepts, but our hearts burst with pleasure when we actually saw evidence of how they actively applied those truths.

When well understood, the law of karma naturally creates good people. This law is the grand equalizer of men. It makes people think twice before uttering unkind words or repeating idle gossip. It makes people honest and trustworthy. It makes people put others first. It makes people less inclined to criticize the actions of others. The law of karma is the most beautiful truth we have, for it gives the foundation of soul justice to all other spiritual concepts.

This latest incident with Sarah was added to all the previous ones our children had created. They showed a remarkable grasp of the difficult concepts, yet this is how it should be with youngsters. Our children have been fortunate enough to have chosen us as their parents. They have grown up with the personal knowledge of the intricate workings of spirit guides. They have been present when such communications had come through, they have conversed with guides. Yes, they notice the change when he manifests and they suddenly become embarrassed when asked a question by the guide, but they are also wild with excited questions of their own making. And they are always answered to their complete satisfaction.

Our girls were becoming more aware as each day passed. Examples of this growing awareness cropped up unexpectedly and were eagerly shared with the rest of the family. One such instance was when Sarah casually mentioned to me that she had seen my spirit during the night.

I was amazed at this new occurrence and I questioned her further. "Tell me about it."

She spoke in a very matter-of-fact tone. "Well, everyone was sleeping and it was real dark. I don't know why I woke up, I just did. And there you were—just standing in my bedroom doorway looking at me."

"How do you know it was me? It could've been your guide. It could've been Jenny walking through the house."

"No, I knew it was you, I could tell. Besides, my guide's a lot taller than you and Jenny was already in bed."

"What did you do when you saw me standing there?"

She grinned with honesty. "At first I thought it was *really* you, you know, your body. And I called out. But when you didn't answer and just stood there . . . well then I pulled the covers over my head."

I laughed and hugged her. "Sarah! You know my spirit wouldn't hurt you, silly."

She smiled wide. "Yeah, I know, but it sure was spooky. Then I peaked over the covers and you were gone. I listened for a minute and then I went into your room, you know, just to make sure."

"And?"

"And you were sound sleep."

"You weren't afraid to walk through the dark house after you saw the spirit?"

"Kindof, but I put the white light around me and, besides, my guide went with me."

Such was Sarah's first spirit sighting. Even though my children have been well versed in the ways of spirits, one's actual first encounter can be a frightening experience, so much so that no matter how well prepared you are, you are likely to forget all your previous learning in deference to fear. It is one thing to believe and talk bravely about it, but it is quite another to actually have a physical encounter.

Bill and I were proud of the way Sarah had handled hers. We were proud of all our girls. They tried so hard at being the right kind of person, the kind God would want His people to be. I only wished that the present day adults could've grown up believing as they did. What a greatly satisfying world we would now have, what a magnificent world! But it hasn't worked out that way. No-Eyes said that the future tribulations of mankind were not going to be caused by God's final wrath, but rather caused by the deepening negative vibrations set up by mankind itself. What have we brought upon ourselves? Now we need to become as the little children; trusting, believing, and filled with unshakable faith.

As I drove to the old woman's cabin, I thought about these things. I felt comforted by my own children's simple acceptance. They didn't need to see to believe, they believed and their spirits naturally became aware enough to see. They believed and they accepted.

I felt uplifted as I parked the truck and hiked up to the lone cabin. No-Eyes was sitting on the porch with several large baskets of piñon cones around her chair. She had been shelling the nuts. "Summer be happy this day, huh."

I grinned. "Yes, I am."

She shrugged. "Summer not gonna tell why?"

My grin widened into a look that bordered on mischief. "You tell me."

"Humph. Summer think No-Eyes got some crystal ball?"

"Yeah, up here," I replied pointing to my head.

She frowned and looked away into the woods. She was intent.

I patiently waited for my teacher to do her mental magic. And without breaking her gaze, she spoke. "It be 'bout Summer's girls. It be 'bout last lesson, lesson 'bout accepting stuff." She turned to me with dancing eyes. "Summer got happy heart 'cause girls accept stuff."

I gave her a disgusted smirk. "Can't I keep *anything* secret? You're too much."

"I not be too much. World no can have too much awareness. Beside, why Summer wanna keep stuff secret anyways?"

"It's not that I want to, No-Eyes. It's just that I never can!"

"No-Eyes not be good teacher if student can hide stuff."

I think she was defending her wise vision ability. "I know that. That's why you're my teacher and I'm just the lowly stumbling student."

She jerked to attention. "Just? Lowly? Summer not be just student here. Summer be *some* student!" She became flustered enough to upset her heaping bowl of piñon nuts.

I ignored the mess. "You're always reminding me that you've never had a student like me. I'm disrespectful when I swear. I'm incorrigible when I tease. I'm inattentive when my mind wanders through the mountains. I'm rude when I make jokes at the wrong times. I'm...."

She stamped her foot. "Stop!"

Silence.

"No-Eyes say Summer be *some* student. No-Eyes mean to say...." She bent her head and retreated within herself.

I saw that she was near tears and I quickly knelt beside her. "And I'm insensitive." I placed my hand over her trembling ones. "I'm sorry I upset you." And I tenderly lifted her chin and searched her dark eyes. "I really am all those things, you know. But even with my teasing, wanderings, and swearing, I've learned more from you than I could've learned from a hundred mountaintop sages. You're the best teacher in the world and...and I love you."

She inhaled a deep breath of mountain air and slowly exhaled as she squeezed my hand. "Summer be like cool rain on dry woods. Summer be No-Eyes' last student. Some days Summer be bad, but it be a refreshing bad for No-Eyes. When Summer leave after lessons, No-Eyes give thanks to Great Spirit for...."

"Thanks?" There were times when I was sure she had deeply regretted the day our paths had crossed.

"Summer interrupt too much even," she grinned. "No-Eyes not finished here. I give thanks to Great Spirit for time He send Summer to No-Eyes' woods. No time ever before No-Eyes get student who question so much. No time before No-Eyes get student who let feelings out so easy. No time student be close like Summer be."

That was quite a mouthful and I knew how hard it was for her to express such deep heartfelt emotions. And now I was the one who had to fight down the hard lump in my throat. All I could do was hug her. I held on tight to my old sightless friend of vision.

Shortly thereafter, she tapped my arms. "We not gonna be good here. We not gonna get lesson done when we all mushy."

I pulled back and gradually firmed up my heart. "Want to go inside now?"

"We gonna go sit by stream today," she announced with a twinkle in her eye.

After I picked up the scattered piñon nuts and cones, we began our descent. "No-Eyes, what is the Phoenix doing now?"

"After he spread wings in and out he gonna stop. He gonna listen hard. He not like what he know coming and he gonna speak. He gonna let out terrible screech noises. He cry in great wail for people's future."

We carefully weaved in and out of some wide squawberry bushes. "Is he crying for the people or for what is happening? What will be happening now?"

"First stuff first. He cry for both peoples and for what he see coming."

We cleared the brilliant red bushes and stepped slowly down through the hillside grass. "And? What will be going on?"

She gripped my arm as she lost her footing and caught herself. "We gonna get down to stream first."

As we made our way toward the twisting stream, I took a selfish delight in the autumn day. A falcon glided effortlessly through his private domain of cobalt blue. His property deed was free and clear. He had no restrictive covenants forced upon his domain. The mighty bird flew through clean and clear skies. I wondered if he knew how fortunate he was. He didn't have to worry about the land grabbers. He didn't have to give a thought to the money-hungry developers who cut and divided the lands like so many soft pieces of pies. And he never cried over the scars that were cruelly carved into the Earth Mother by the mining operations. No, the falcon was carefree in his beautiful domain that no man could ever lay claim to, no man could ever take away from him, no man could ever desecrate. I watched his wondrous flight and wished that I could be like him.

Suddenly my arm was roughly jerked and I was quickly brought back to the present.

"Summer, that be no good."

"I know," I admitted dejectedly, "but it's not right. The land doesn't belong to our Earth Mother anymore."

She clicked her tongue. "No can change stuff. Summer not think 'bout sad stuff like that. Beside, we here at stream now. Sit down. I gonna tell 'bout Phoenix days, days when he gonna wail loud over all lands."

I helped the old one get settled on a soft area of grass beside the rushing watercourse and I brushed aside some twigs that were scattered over my own spot.

It was a beautiful place for our talk. The sunlight fell softly through the forest and it made me think of the happier times when we were here. Suddenly No-Eyes held up an extended finger and I watched joyfully as an iridescent green and red hummingbird landed momentarily before it noisily sped off in search of a more nourishing landing pad. We laughed at the tiny humorous bird.

The old woman leaned forward to rest her elbows on her crossed legs. She wasn't going to waste any time. "Phoenix be ready to warn. Phoenix gonna screech loud and long. His wail gonna come same time as nuclear stuff."

"No nuclear war. Not the short exchange."

She played with her fingernails. "Nope. That be later. Summer, peoples stupid. They got live stuff buried inside Earth Mother. She no like that stuff. It hurt her bad, it burn her real bad. Earth Mother cry in pain. She gonna try to get rid of bad burning stuff peoples put there. She gonna *do* it too."

"Wait. We need to get the right words here. You said 'live' stuff that burns. . . ."

"Yup. No-Eyes mean nuclear stuff that burn Earth Mother. What Summer's word for that?"

"Radiation. Radioactive materials and waste."

"That what No-Eyes mean. Yup." She appeared to be listening to the stream before speaking again. "Earth Mother sick and tired of peoples burning waste in her breast. She gonna give it back to peoples. She gonna show peoples how bad she hurt. She give peoples back their own bad medicine even." She pursed her lips and nodded with a glowing self satisfaction.

I wasn't so elated with the Earth Mother's intended revenge. I could clearly understand it but I wasn't pleased like my teacher obviously was. "Is the earth going to have quakes at the dump sites?"

"Two spots only."

"How many areas will this affect altogether?"

"Ten, maybe twelve even."

"Populated areas?"

"Some gonna be."

"If two will have quakes, what will the others have? What will they seep from?"

She shrugged uncaringly. "They just gonna ooze up."

"Just? No-Eyes, how can you be so casual about this? If toxic waste is going to leach back up to the surface, then hundreds of people will be in terrible danger."

"More even."

"Thousands?"

She simply nodded.

"I can't believe you're so uncaring about this. Before, you've always shown such empathy for the people. Why are you suddenly pulling a switch?"

She smiled. "No-Eyes not pull no switch. No-Eyes all time feel good 'bout this one stuff. Peoples dumb. They finally gonna get back what they cause on Earth Mother."

"But the general *public* didn't cause the material to be dumped in the Earth Mother. The *people* don't have anything to say about it. Why should they have to be the ones to suffer for the harmful acts of others?"

"It no matter *what* peoples do the dump stuff. What matter here be that the dump stuff be *done*. The act itself be what important here."

"Not to me. I don't see the justice."

"There *be* no justice done to Earth Mother! Huh, Summer, where justice there? Listen, if Summer get hurt bad by people, Summer try to heal hurt no matter what people do that hurt. See? The healing what most important."

"Yeah, but I don't strike back at innocent people for my hurts either."

"Summer no strike anyways. But first Summer try to heal hurt. Right?"

"Yes."

"That all Earth Mother gonna try too. She send burning stuff back up out of scarred breast. That all. She not mean to hurt back peoples— only get rid of stuff that hurt."

"But before, you sounded like she would be taking revenge on the people. You said she'd give them their own bad medicine back. That certainly sounds like a purposeful action of retaliation to me."

"Earth Mother only get rid of stuff. No-Eyes be one who say she gonna give back peoples own medicine, Earth Mother not say that."

"Then you're pleased with this future event."

Silence.

I couldn't comprehend my friend being pleased by any such dreaded catastrophe. In the past she had maintained a sympathetic and even a tearful attitude whenever we spoke of the disasters that were to befall mankind. "You *are* pleased!"

She didn't like my shocked reaction. She threw her arms up and began ranting. "What Earth Mother s'posed to *do*? Peoples think they so *smart!* They think they so *advanced!* They advance right into own made *disaster! Peoples* be *dumb*, Summer. *Peoples* be *stupid* dumb with *advance* stuff! They no *see!* They no *see* stuff they *do* even!"

I didn't want this. She was difficult to bring down from one of her tirades once she began them. "No-Eyes, please," I tried.

"No-Eyes be *right!* No-Eyes got *right* to anger! Summer think *Indian* Peoples do stuff like *white* peoples do to Earth Mother? *Indian* be full of *love* for her. *They* no *hurt* her. *They* no *burn, scar!*"

I understood her deep-rooted feelings and I spoke softly. "I know, but the Indian People are no longer the nation of the land and . . . ."

She suddenly altered her mood. The lady relaxed and let a slow knowledgeable grin creep across her face. "Summer say funny stuff. I gonna say something here too. It be for last lesson, but I gonna say something 'cause Summer bring stuff up now." She paused to raise her time wrinkled face to the sun. And turning with beaming pride written all over it, she whispered. "Summer, Indian nation gonna rise up again like great Phoenix do. Indian nation gonna be as one! It gonna be *strong* like before."

My heart raced with each quiet word she uttered. "But how. . . ."

Her finger went up to thin lips. "No-Eyes say that stuff be for *last* lesson."

And I grinned. "You're teasing me. You're *baiting* me!"

Her sharp chin shot up into the air. "Nope. Summer bring up stuff here. No-Eyes only correct Summer's false idea."

"Can't you tell me just a little bit? Please?" I pleaded.

"We not gonna get stuff mixed up here. We gonna talk 'bout nuclear stuff today."

And that was her final word about that. The subject of the rise of the Indian nation was definitely closed until she alone deemed the proper time to reopen it again.

I felt deflated at having to waste this magnificent autumn day talking about nuclear waste leakage when we could be discussing happier topics. However, we didn't see eye-to-eye and whenever that happened—I lost.

"So!" she began. "Earth Mother gonna dump burn stuff back up into peoples' face. That be only start. . . ."

"Wonderful," I mumbled sarcastically.

Brown hand cupped behind a brown ear. "No-Eyes hear smart mouth again?"

"No. Not really. I simply don't see how it can get much worse because now you say that the leaching is just the *beginning*!"

"Yup. That be right. Summer maybe not want to hear, but Summer gonna listen anyways."

"Do I have a choice?"

She flashed me one of her disgusted bad student stares.

"Oh all right, go ahead."

"Humph. That more like it. Big nuclear plants gonna get close to danger. Summer give word for that stuff."

I thought about what she might mean by danger and I explained what a meltdown was.

"That be right word. All plants not gonna do that stuff but they gonna get close—real close."

"In populated areas?"

105

"Some gonna be."

"Will these near accidents cause people to take a second look at the nuclear plants? Will they be closed down?"

She merely shook her head.

"Oh for God's sake! What next?" I muttered disgustedly.

She took my comment to be literal. "Next Phoenix gonna screech when other burn stuff leak out. He gonna. . . ."

"Wait! *What* other burn stuff? *Different* radioactive material?"

"Yup. This be war stuff."

She had to mean chemical warfare materials. Or maybe highly radioactive weapons. And my first thought sped like an arrow toward the Rocky Mountain Arsenal. Even though my heart raced, I tried to appear calm. "No-Eyes, you wouldn't by any chance mean that something will happen at the Rocky Mountain Arsenal." And I really didn't want to hear the answer. I already knew what it was going to be.

"Yup."

"There's going to be an accident?"

"Earth Mother gonna be upset. She gonna shake it bad."

"An earthquake?"

She merely shrugged her shoulders and looked up through the dense trees.

"I have the distinct feeling that that's for another day."

"Yup."

"So, something's going to shake the arsenal and cause a radio-active material and chemical release, but you won't say *what* will actually cause the shaking until another lesson."

"Summer got stuff right here."

"Tomorrow."

"Yup. But we got one more stuff for today. Summer, there gonna be nuclear leak stuff happen, but there also gonna be two last big ones go off. They be in spots where many peoples be. They gonna get many peoples."

My heart sunk with a deafening thud. She had indeed saved the absolute worst for last. "*Real* meltdowns?"

And the deadly silence that followed said it all.

Talons Tensing

*And the youngling kneaded its
mighty talons deep into the
soft yielding breast of its
Earth Mother.*

After my disturbing afternoon with the old woman, I desperately craved the normalcy of family distractions. I couldn't live with the knowledge that had been shared with me that day. I had entertained thoughts of driving up to my sacred ground to be alone in order to reason out my lesson, but then I thought better of the idea and decided to return home to the irritating sounds that occasionally drove me right up the wall.

When I entered the house, the television blared a football game. Bill and Jenny were jumping up and down shouting out plays to our losing team. Aimee's stereo was shaking her bedroom walls and Sarah was bitterly complaining that the dog was always finding her hiding places too soon.

I found the total commotion to be oddly welcomed. I had found exactly what I needed, just what the doctor ordered—mental distractions.

I put Rainbow, the dog, back outside. And I kept her out until Sarah had excitedly found the perfect hiding place—one that the dog would never find. Finally, when given the go-ahead, I let Rainbow back in and instructed her to go find Sarah. I laughed, as she went right to her. She was always easy, because she never failed to giggle wildly whenever the dogs sniffed around her hiding place. Then, in their glee, both dog and girl rolled about on the floor in a new game of wrestling. Again, the dog always won.

We repeated the Hide and Seek game until it was time for Sarah to begin winding down before bedtime, then she and I played Rummy until she got bored with beating her poor ol' mom. I think she felt sorry for me. She didn't voice those sentiments and I didn't mention that I had *let* her win.

The activity of playing with the girls and helping them get ready for bed brought on a physical and mental tiredness. I tucked Sarah and Aimee into their king-sized bed. Sarah gave me a bear hug and asked me if I'd tuck in the quilt on her side. This was a new request.

"Why do you want the quilt tucked in?" I asked.

"So no skeletony hands can reach up and grab me."

I looked down at the floor where she kept her assortment of stuffed animals heaped in a mountainous pile. "Don't you think your zoo will protect you?"

She shook her head and long golden hair swished from side to side. "No silly, my *guide* does that!"

"Then what's the deal with the quilt?"

"That's just double protection. This way, I help her protect me."

I smiled at her childlike coverup. Of course I knew what was pestering her little mind, she had been to the movies today. "You wouldn't by any chance think there's a stray gremlin around would you?"

She was mildly outraged. "I'm too old to believe in that!"

"That's what I thought." And I kissed her goodnight after making sure the quilt was tucked in extra tight.

Aimee was next. I skirted around the large bed to her side. She winked knowingly and snickered quietly at her sister's pretended bravery. "Mom, I love you so much," she said as she squeezed the air out of me, "don't ever leave."

I squeezed back. "I won't if I can help it, honey."

"I hope God never calls you before me."

I pulled back and held up her chin. "That's not a very happy thought just before bed. Aimee, nobody knows what's in God's mind. All we can do is love each other each day."

She was very concerned with this line of thought. "Why don't more people do that?"

"Do what?"

"Well, like you always say, treat each other like they know the other guy was going to die tomorrow. Why aren't people nice to each other?"

"Because they have a free will, remember? Even though they know in their hearts what's right, they can still choose which way to act. Now, what's this all about?"

"Well, the news is full of murder and stuff like that. . . . "

"Aimee, all you have to worry about is how Aimee treats people. Those others on television will have to answer for their own bad deeds. Now, you leave that ugly business to those on the otherside and don't worry your pretty little head about it anymore. Hear me?"

"Yeah, but I still want God to take me first."

I smoothed the covers up around her shoulders. "I think it'd be better if you thought more about living than dying."

"It'd be a better place to live if more people thought about dying and what their record's going to look like."

She had a point. And I kissed her after telling her to imagine a beautiful place to meet her guide at.

Jenny was too big to be tucked in. She came into her sisters' room to tell me goodnight. She put her arms around me and innocently said, "I don't ever want things to change."

These morbid moods were becoming contagious. "Things are always changing, Jenny."

"I mean us," she clarified.

"Things around us will change, but we'll still be together."

She was satisfied with that and went off to bed. Then she hollered back, "Mom, I'm glad you know things."

I wasn't. "I'm glad you're glad, honey, sweet dreams." And I joined Bill in the living room.

He set the paper down and patted his lap. "What'd the wise one have to say today? Anything good?"

"That depends on what you mean by good. Seems one man's grief is another's joy."

He looked puzzled. "She happy or sad?"

I got up and headed toward the kitchen. "I don't want to talk about it."

He followed on my heels. "Hey! Since when don't we talk?" As always, he was concerned about my feelings. He pulled me to him. "Come on, what's the matter? What'd she say now?"

I had a bad habit of slamming down a steel shell over my tender emotions when I didn't want to discuss something sensitive. It was an unjust and cruel way to treat someone I loved, but it was my only defense against being forced to talk about painful matters. Bill had become adept at cracking that shell and I hoped that he wouldn't try tonight because I always ended up crying when the defense was broken. Only Bill could bring up the out-pouring of my deeply repressed emotions.

I held hard and cold against his attempt. "Nothing!" I barked.

"You were out there *all* afternoon and she never *spoke?* She never said *anything?*"

I exasperatedly shifted my weight. "Do you *have* to know *everything?*"

He held me to him. Damn! He was going to do it. He stroked my hair. "Honey, please, I love you so much. Don't keep the hurt inside. Don't shut me out."

Everything would've been fine if only he had shouted back at me. I could handle arguing—tenderness I couldn't. I hated it when he became extra gentle when I was forcing the opposite outward feelings, I just hated it. "I just don't want to talk about it right now." And I stiffly bristled in his arms.

He was stubborn. He hugged all the harder. "Mary, I love you, please talk to me, please honey," he softly whispered into my ear.

The lump lodged. The eyes began to sting. Shoulders trembled. My shell cracked wide open and fell in pieces about my feet.

He cradled me in his arms as he led me into our room.

I poured out my depressing day and we talked. We talked for a long while before we fell silent. We looked hard into each other's eyes and soon we were the only two people in the entire world. He had shattered my emotional shell and had made my world beautiful with his love. I slept like a newborn babe.

Then, bulbous red eyes blinked before me. Deafening squawking sounds pierced the night's stillness and my eyes flew open. I was dreaming of the Phoenix and I was frightened. I looked over to Bill for comfort. "Bill?" I whispered. He moaned and turned away. I was foolish to waken him. What could he possibly do?"

The Phoenix days were invading my sleep. I was half expecting this. I tried to get comfortable again. I tried to concentrate on happier thoughts. Isn't that what I had told Aimee to do earlier? I tossed again and again, yet every time I closed my eyes, the great Phoenix was crouching there—glaring back at me with flaring red eyes that darted wildly about.

This was getting ridiculously out of hand. I had better mental control than this! I rolled on my back and ran a blank film through my mind's eye. Soon, I felt the familiar weaving sensations, the weightlessness, then nothing but sweet oblivion.

Bird claws as monstrous as houses grabbed into the soft earth. The leg's muscular tendons strained as the scaled toes curled their yellow talons deeply into the living soil. Great rents ripped through the ground. The razor talons sliced deep trenches each time they cruelly clutched at the soil. Gushers of vermilion spewed up from beneath the claws and rivers of blood pulsed forth. The feet lifted and curled into new sections of soil, tearing and ripping as the massive toes restlessly

110

kneaded their talons unmercifully into the Earth Mother's tender breast. And the fresh blood flowed darkly over all the land.

Cities were in shambles from crazed rioting crowds. All minorities were taking revenge upon the unjust world. Buildings were crackling as hellish flames hungrily licked and gutted. Windows were blown out. Explosions ripped. Groups of angry weapon-wielding gangs roamed the rubble-littered streets in search for someone to take their madness out on. Sirens pierced the deafening din. Guns cracked. Laughter of the insane rang in my ears. I ran to an alleyway and slushed through its wet darkness. When I came to an unbroken streetlamp, I saw that I had been trampling through blood, blood bright and thick. I swung around just in time to see it all vanish within the blinding flash of a mushroom cloud. And I released all my remaining energy in a soundless scream.

I awoke with beads of sweat clinging coldly to my forehead. My palms were clammy. I peered over at Bill, no, I wouldn't wake him. I left the quiet bedroom and squinted up at the schoolhouse clock that ticked against the kitchen wall. I saw that it was three in the morning. I should've known what time it was—my magic dream hour was always around three.

I brought the kerosene lantern to life and warmed to the soft glow that filled the big country kitchen. And lighting a cigarette, I sat at the table while I thought about my awful nightmare. It had terrified me. A shiver rippled over the surface of my bare shoulders. Shivers drifted in and out with the thoughts like three-dimensional movie effects that were cleverly designed to scare the hell out of the audience.

I reviewed the dreadful visual scenes until I could rationally decipher the dream symbols. The clock pendulum swung in time to my methodic thoughts. It ticked the seconds away. It ticked toward my future.

I mentally made all the correct interpretations but I couldn't reach the logical associations and reasoning for them. I never had trouble with dream symbols before. This one was most bewildering.

Tick-tock. Tick-tock.

Then I realized why the symbols made no corresponding sense—they weren't symbols at all, they were real! I shuddered at the mere thought of having once again dreamed of a future event. The precognitive dreams were nothing unusual to speak of, but I shivered this time because of *what* I had dreamed.

I lit another cigarette and watched the blue smoke swirl up from the glowing tip while I reviewed the things I had learned in my recent weekends with my old sage. I had almost come to detest my visits with No-Eyes lately because of the depressing subject matters of the lessons. I couldn't help the feeling of hatred that slept just beneath the surface of my heart whenever I thought of the Phoenix. Even though I knew that he wasn't the actual cause of the terrible changes to come, I sensed a subliminal sort of satisfied justice emitting from his mind. He was still too closely connected with the future to completely disengage himself from it.

Then my mind wandered to the mention No-Eyes had made of the rise of the Indian nation. I couldn't logically conceive how this wondrous, but seemingly impossible, event could come to be. But, if she foresaw it, I faithfully believed it. Perhaps the Phoenix was going to herald in a new civilization of aware people. This new idea enlightened my spirit. Perhaps when all has been destroyed and purified, the new nation would then thrive as God had originally intended mankind to. It would certainly be a new beginning. Yes, maybe this Phoenix would wipe the slate clean, clear away the deadwood to allow room for the new peaceful age of awareness to grow and flourish strong in the sunlight, thrive to build their new world on the foundation of oneness with the Earth Mother.

Then again, that might only be conjecture. Yet, out of all my viable present options, I held firm with my assumption, returned to bed and soundly slept until Rainbow nudged my cheek in the morning.

It was late. I was late. This day I was supposed to join the medicine woman in the sacred rite of our Daybreak Benediction. But I had thoughtlessly overslept. She would be furious, or worse yet, give her delinquent student the old frigid shoulder.

I frantically pulled on my jeans and a flannel shirt, grabbed my serape, let the dog out—back in, and left the house.

Driving through Woodland was frustrating because I couldn't push over the speed limit, but once I cleared the outskirts, I sped down the deserted sideroads through the National Forest until I reached the clearing near her cabin. Breathlessly I raced up the hill and through her creaky door.

She had been concentrating on measuring out the proper mixture of one of her special herbal formulas. Without breaking her intense mental calculations, she barked at me. "That door gonna break yet! Get over here. I gonna show Summer new medicine stuff today."

I couldn't believe my ears. She hadn't been upset with me for being late, for missing our hilltop prayer ceremony. Today was supposed to be another dreadful lesson of the Phoenix chronicles, and I was elated that she had changed the lesson plan. I removed my heavy blanket wrap and joined her in the tiny kitchen. "What are you making?" I asked curiously while peering at the various stoppered containers.

She made meticulous measurements with her fingers before

pouring the exact proportions into an oddly shaped jar. "This gonna help Summer sleep better." She knew of my bad night.

I examined the side of her creviced face while she worked. "So you know."

"Yup. Teacher be no good if she not keep close eye on student." She returned the stray containers to her massive supply cabinet, came back to the table and pushed a cork stopper into the apothecary jar before handing it to me. "There, Summer steep one-fourth teaspoon in cup of tea before bed."

I scrutinized the curious contents of the green glass jar. "One quarter? That's not very much!" I exclaimed as I shook the powdery mixture. Then my fingers began to tingle with kinetic energy.

She pointed a warning finger and tapped the glass. "Summer *no* take *more*! Summer take more, maybe Summer not ever wake up!"

I returned my gaze to the mysterious concoction. And I knew she had used some of her narcotic plants. She had formulated my sleeping potion in an incredibly strong dose. "Maybe I'll only take half the signature," I mused.

"Summer take what No-Eyes say. This stuff be powerful, it need be taken in exact amount here!"

"Okay . . . but I don't think I'll need the whole jar. There's enough in this to put the lights out of the entire town!"

She gently placed her hand over mine. "Summer take. That stuff never go bad. Someday maybe Summer find good need for it, help peoples with it."

And my heart fluttered with her words. I was about to object when she stopped me cold. "Summer think she know stuff she not ever have to do. Summer not realize how she gonna help peoples in future. Stuff gonna be bad for peoples. Peoples gonna hurt so bad they never gonna get better. This stuff gonna ease suffering of dying peoples, see?" Her fingers caressed the jar I held. "Summer take for good sleep now. Then—Summer have stuff for later help too."

I looked down at the green jar, then my eyes locked onto hers. "Thank you, No-Eyes." And I thought I caught a wet glisten in the dark pools before she turned and shuffled off into the living room.

I watched as she fussed with the rocker and sat in it. Creak-thud. Creak-thud.

A sudden chill rippled down my back. "How about I make us a cozy fire? Would you like that?"

She sighed deeply. "That be nice, Summer."

The wood had been recently stacked and I picked out several small pieces of aspen and added them to the dry juniper kindling. Soon the crackling and flickering flames sent radiating beams of warmth into the room. A sweet scent wafted lazily over our heads. I topped off the pile with a couple of applewood branches that her friends had given her and I sat on the couch by my friend.

She was sullen.

"What's the matter?" I quietly asked.

Creak-thud. Creak-thud.

The chill was leaving the room, yet the cabin darkened with the ominous effects of gathering thunderheads. We were going to have another one of our famous autumn Rocky Mountain thunderstorms. I thought about how the storms had recently increased in their intensity. It was as if more energy was being released from them. The rain now fell with the force of javelins being thrown down and the thunder was deafening as it cracked and echoed endlessly between the mountain ranges.

Creak-thud. Creak-thud.

I returned my attention to my friend. She was staring at me. "No-Eyes be sorry to give Summer bad dream stuff."

"You didn't do that. You simply relayed what you foresaw. I let it get to me, that's all."

She solemnly shook her head. "Summer no understand stuff here. We s'posed to talk more 'bout nuclear stuff this day."

"And we will," I encouraged.

"Summer still not get it. When Summer have this bad dream?"

"Last night."

"Night?"

"Well, actually it was around three in the . . . morning—today," came the sinking reality.

Creak-thud.

She *did* do it. She had given my lesson already. "Why'd you do it that way. Couldn't it have waited for today—during the day?"

She inclined her shoulders toward me. "We talk 'bout future stuff. We talk and talk some more even. Summer, talk be only words. Some stuffs not mean much if they only be words, see?"

"You mean that I needed to actually *see*, to *feel* the future in order to grasp its gravity?"

"Yup, that be needed here."

"But I *do* grasp its gravity. No-Eyes, these things we've been discussing are nothing less than horrendous! Of all people, you should know that I've been taking all of this very seriously. Don't you think I have a good enough imagination to visualize these things? Why do you think I need to unload the pain and suffering I feel for the future?"

She leaned back. "No-Eyes know all that stuff. No-Eyes not be dumb teacher."

"I wasn't inferring that you were."

Creak-thud. "Summer need to see stuff here, that all. We speak now 'bout stuff in dream."

"Do we have to? It really was visual enough."

"Not 'nough. Summer miss some stuff. We gonna talk now."

Rolling thunder rattled the frail cabin with deep resonating vibrations while my determined teacher gathered her thoughts. "Who Summer see in dream streets?"

"The people were a mixture of minorities."

She hesitated noticeably as if having second thoughts about what to say next. Then she continued. "What these peoples do in dream?"

"They were rioting. They were angry, insane with anger. They roamed about in large groups with clubs, axes, guns—anything they could use as a weapon or tool of destruction."

"But why Summer?"

"I suppose they were revolting against injustices done to them. They probably had had enough suppression and they decided to take matters into their own hands."

"That be true, but Summer still leave out why. Besides," she paused "there be *white* peoples in those gangs in dream even. Summer not take time to see those peoples. Summer try too hard to hide in alley first."

'I thought the gang represented the minorities."

"That be true too. This time *all* peoples be minor peoples." She was quickly losing me in the forest of her words. "How can that be? I mean, who's left to be superior?"

Her brows furrowed together. "State peoples, Summer."

"The government?"

She spoke softly as she again bent toward me. "Listen Summer, this be most important stuff here. State peoples first gonna make two or three bad laws for peoples. People not gonna have say 'bout these laws. These laws be made in big building in state."

"Hold on. We need to clarify this. I know whenever you use the word state, you mean the government. So, the government will make a few laws without the people voting on them. That's clear. But this big building in the government, I'm not sure about. Can you give me more information here?"

She though, then added, "There be seven or eight men in dark dresses."

"Could there be women in this group? Could there be as many as nine people in long black robes?"

She checked. "Yup, women too even. Summer be right. There be nine."

"No-Eyes, those people are called the Supreme Court Justices. They pass laws that govern the entire country." I thought a minute. "And you're saying that they'll be passing laws that aren't good for the people."

"That right."

"But two or three laws don't incite massive riots."

"No-Eyes not done speakin' here. No-Eyes say *first* two or three. But they gonna make many more bad laws for peoples. They make laws to take away peoples' private life, private rights to *spirit* ways, private everything even!"

"That would leave us with a police state! Are you absolutely certain about this?"

"Yup, No-Eyes certain. Summer keep eye on this court, watch all laws it gonna make. It gonna look like no big thing at first, but it gonna get more and more strong over peoples private stuff."

My mental vision wandered through the terrible scenes of the dream. "It's going to be a nightmare. I can see why the people were rioting. No-Eyes, is this sort of public reaction going to go on all over or is it going to be centered in one or two specific big cities?"

Eyes twinkled. "It gonna be all over. It gonna go on over all land. But it gonna be start of finish."

The mushroom cloud rose sickeningly clear. "What will the nuclear explosion be from?"

"Summer remember we talk 'bout burning stuff that Earth Mother gonna push back up?"

"Yeah," I admitted hesitantly.

"And remember that Summer tell No-Eyes to fill in missing part, gap in story?"

"Yes. That was the part about the chemical weapons arsenal. You were going to tell me how it shakes...."

She winked.

"But you also said *shake*, not *explode*!"

"It shake *first, then* it blow up to sky."

I felt we were playing word games again, more accurately, thought games. "I'm going to try to put this out on the table, No-Eyes. You're drawing this out too long. I'm going to just say what I think you're getting at, but I want you to stop me if I'm wrong."

Creak-thud.

"I think the Earth Mother will quake and cause seepage of radioactive waste, a few nuclear plants will get close to having accidents, two will actually have a total meltdown and then..." I hesitated out of uncertainty, "and then the nucluear war exchange will occur. One will strike New York City and one will strike the arsenal and

116

blow it away." There, I had said it. Right or wrong, I spoke my theory. Silence.

I waited for comment. I waited for a firm confirmation or denial. Silence.

"Well?"

"Well what? Summer tell No-Eyes to speak if Summer be wrong. I no speak."

I wished she had. "Then I'm right."

"Did No-Eyes stop Summer?"

No comment.

"Why Summer not talk? Summer got right idea here."

"I don't feel like talking."

She stiffened angrily. "Summer maybe can pull that stuff on Bill—no can pull on No-Eyes! We gonna talk anyways!"

So I did. "Who sends these missiles, bombs?"

Her bottom lip shoved out and curled under. "That not be important here...."

I disagreed. "*I* think it *is*! Who *sends* them, No-Eyes?"

Silence. She wasn't going to answer. She rocked until I cooled, then she leaned forward to place her hand on my lap.

"What be important here, Summer? Think 'bout spirit lessons before Summer answer."

I didn't have to do any thinking about them because I already knew. "Cleaning up, the *caring* for the survivors will be what's most important—the healing."

She patted my knee. I was a good little obedient student. "That right. It no matter *who* do bad hurt, what matter be the *healing.*"

I looked outside and watched the storm clouds break up. Mankind had to emulate nature. She could be furiously devastating with droughts, then she refreshed and made life well once again with her rain. The sun peered down between the drifting clouds and shot its bright rays through the thin curtains. "You're right," I conceded, "people will have to join in aiding others, that's most important."

The old one suddenly rose from the chair. "Summer, No-Eyes got some friends that gonna come here soon. We no talk more today. Summer go home with family now. We all done this day."

"Is it personal? Couldn't I stay to meet them?"

"Summer could, but No-Eyes want Summer be with family. Summer need break here."

That was true, but I was undecided in what I wished to do. I wanted to leave, yet I didn't. "They'll understand. I could stay for a while longer."

She held out my serape. "Too much bad future talk no good.

Family have happy hearts when Summer be home early."

I felt like I was being evicted. "I guess you're right. I really could use a Sunday afternoon away from this mess." And I hugged the small woman before going to the door.

"Summer?" she softly called.

I turned. She had the apothecary jar in her hand. "Forgot something."

I took the jar and opened the door. "No-Eyes?"

"Yup?"

"I love you."

Silence.

The narrow mountain roads were awash with orange mud, they were deeply cut by the runoff rivulets of rainwater that had carved shortcuts across them. It had evidently rained harder than I had thought. When I reached the mainstreet of Woodland, it too was covered with a blanket of dirt that had been carried across the road by waters gushing through town. This was usual after a hard rainfall, for Woodland Park was situated on a mountain Pass. When the storms raged, the water rushed down the mountainsides and through the dirt roads. And by the amount of dirt on the street, Woodland had received the worst of the storm.

I pulled into the garage and, before I could get out of the truck, Jenny and Rainbow were there to greet me. We entered the house and I was attacked by an excited family. Bill was concerned that I was home so early. After satisfying him that everything was all right, we decided to take a shopping trip down to Colorado Springs and have a pizza dinner.

We enjoyed our afternoon together, for they were excited that No-Eyes had given me the extra time with them. On our way back up the Pass, we stopped off at one of our friend's house and stayed until it was Sarah's bedtime. It had been a busy day for everyone and the girls were relieved to hit the sack. I was tired too, but Bill had other plans. "Let's go for a walk."

My body wanted to refuse, but it had been a while since we had walked around the neighborhood at night, so I agreed. And after giving Jenny the usual babysitting instructions, we left.

It was dark, yet the moon shone brightly and reflected the sparkles of glistening raindrops off the wavering pines. The air held a refreshing scent of newness. Here and there, a trail of woodsmoke curled lazily up out of chimneys and I imagined the crackling voice of the people's friendly fires.

Our walks were good, they soothed the weary spirit and gave an invigorating energy to the physical. We used to take them every evening, but since school began, we were usually too busy helping the girls with their homework. We were glad this had been Sunday. We were glad to be outside in the crisp autumn evening once again. The neighborhood was silent and our footfalls upon the damp earthen road were barely audible.

Some nights we walked for an hour without either of us speaking. We'd simply hold hands and let our love for each other pulse through the clasped bond. "This was a nice idea," I said quietly trying not to shatter the stillness.

"It's been a while."

"Yeah, too bad we get so busy."

We strolled another block before he spoke again. "Since you're not saying much about your morning, I gather you don't want to talk about it."

I shrugged. "No, it's okay. I was just enjoying this—it's so peaceful."

"It's okay," he said, "we really should be doing this back up in the mountains though. I know how much you miss our old place."

I did miss that little log cabin, but I also knew that one day we'd get a place of our own with miles of treed mountains for neighbors. "Someday we'll have our own place up there to walk around in. This'll do for now."

"So, if you don't mind talking, what went on this morning?"

She made me a special formula. Remind me to get it out of the camper when we get back. It's to help me sleep better. It's got powerful substances in it so I'll have to explain it to the girls."

He frowned. "They never touch any of your concoctions."

I raised a brow. "This isn't just an ordinary mixture," I hesitated, "it's got some of her poisonous plants in it—it's potential is deadly."

He broke our steady pace. "Why do we need that?"

I explained the medicine woman's reasoning and he agreed that it was possible that the formula could be of use in the future. I finished relaying my lesson, then brought up my bad night. "I had another nightmare last night but I didn't want to wake you."

"I told you to always get me up whenever you had one of those! Why didn't you?"

"Because there was nothing you could do," I soothed. "Besides, when I realized that it was literal, there was nothing *to* do. So I went back to bed and slept until Bo woke me up. Anyway, the old one talked about my dream. Guess what?"

He chuckled. "You've got to be joking. I could never guess anything you two talk about. Save me the trouble. Enlighten me."

"*She* sent the dream."

His mouth dropped. "Again? She wasn't supposed to *do* that anymore."

"I know, but she said that I needed to actually see things."

"Can't say that I agree with that. Trouble is, you see things too clearly as it is."

"Not always, seems I still missed a few important points." I explained about the minorities, then about the nuclear missile.

He thoughtfully kicked at a rock in the road. "I suppose she didn't bother saying where it came from."

"No." I knew what he was thinking and I had hoped he wouldn't verbalize it.

He did anyway. "Think we could find out?" He was fishing for permission to ask his guide for the missing information.

I feebly attempted to sidestep the issue. "You know you can always ask, but you don't always get the answer you want. I suppose he'd just say the same thing she said."

"No, I think he'll tell us. He rarely conceals facts like that, especially if I ask him straight out."

I was tired and didn't want to be bothered with this sort of thing tonight. I simply wanted to continue enjoying our walk. "I'm awfully tired," I hedged.

He pushed. "Just for a minute?"

I sighed. I couldn't deny him his closest information source, his nebulous buddy. I mentally switched gears and immediately felt the dizzying effect begin to swirl within my consciousness.

The next thing I knew, we were getting ready for bed. "He was here longer than a minute," I teasingly admonished.

Bill grinned sheepishly. "He had a lot to say. So happens there's a twist to this missile thing. Want to hear?"

I remembered the old woman's words about the healing being most important. "I don't think so, not yet anyway." I crawled into bed, kissed him, and switched out the light.

Crouching

*The young bird craned forward into
a low crouch and prepared to leave
its torn birthland.*

I had allowed the entire week to slip by without asking Bill about his private conversation the night we went for our walk. Knowing things was such a heavy burden and I didn't feel that finding out what country was going to bomb us was something I needed to know. We were being fed information from both sides of our world and even though both sources always cross-referenced without discrepancies, I had to draw a line.

It required a firm hold on present realities to be able to handle the complexities of such communications of spiritual knowledge. In order for me to accomplish this, I had to regulate my informational intake. I was always given the free will option to listen in on the discussion or to leave entirely. Mostly, I exercised that free choice by leaving. Bill would then reiterate the information whenever I was ready to discuss it.

So I left the subject alone and headed out once again to my friend's cabin. This was to be my last weekend on the subject of the rising of the great Phoenix. I was anxious to get it over with.

I slowed the truck to allow myself more leisure time to appreciate the changing mood of nature. It was October now and the torrential rains of last weekend had stripped many of the aspens of their golden treasures. The signs were all there. They forewarned of an early winter and I looked forward to the scent of woodsmoke that would hang in our home. For me, each season had its own magnificence. Each season brought with it sights, sounds and scents that permeated my entire being with a total appreciation of life.

Yes, I knew things, terrible things, but was that sufficient reason to ignore the undulating universe I saw thriving within a golden aspen leaf? Was that reason to ignore the tremendous beauty of the mountain sunsets? No, I refused to ignore the Earth Mother's intense riches. The world would experience its worst, but she would also survive, she'll be beautiful once again and I will once again give thanks for that lasting beauty.

I arrived at No-Eyes' cabin and stood by the truck reviewing my purpose. The sun was strong on my face. The hillsides sparkled with dew. The resident falcon glided effortlessly over the deep valley. And I became at ease with my relation to its totality. I did love life.

"Summer gonna stand down there all day?" the old woman yodeled from the doorway.

I looked up the hill toward the cabin. She was impatiently standing on the porch and shouting at me to get on with it. Yes, I loved life. "I'm coming!" I shouted back as I began walking up to greet her.

"We not gonna need fire today. It be plenty warm in here." She closed the door after I entered. "No-Eyes gonna shut *own* door so Summer no *break* it."

I silently chuckled at her humorously rude ways. The rocker was in place by the couch and we assumed our usual places. "Summer take sleep stuff-No-Eyes give?"

"I haven't needed it yet."

"That be good. It still be there though."

"Well," I began, "is this going to take long today?"

"Humph! Summer got somewhere else to go?"

I felt relaxed. I grinned. "No, of course not, I just wondered if this last lessson was going to be a long one."

"That depend. Maybe it be long, maybe it gonna be short. We see how many questions Summer gonna have first."

A logical answer.

I started out with my usual question. "So, what's the bird doing now?"

She exasperatedly clicked her tongue at my flippant disrespect. "He not be *any* bird! He be great Phoenix!"

"I didn't mean it the way it sounded," I defended.

"Summer need to listen to what she say, how stuff be said."

This I knew too well. I was forever being reminded about my off-the-cuff comments. I had done rather well in controlling them. I had come a long way since meeting my teacher, yet there were instances when I was relaxed enough to let them slip out. "I know, I'm sorry."

"Blah! Summer not sorry. Summer think stuff be *funny* here."

And I laughed. "You're my teacher. You know me better than I know myself."

She puffed up at the compliment. "Lucky for Summer. Now great Phoenix gonna crouch down like this." She bent forward and stretched her neck out low. "See?" She looked more like a hungry turtle.

I snickered at the thought.

And she straightened her back. "This not be joke stuff here!"

"I know," I replied without apologizing. Instead, I pasted a serious face over the grin.

"We gonna waste all day here if we not get down to serious minds." The medicine woman paused to eye me with caution. "Now, Phoenix crouch down low. He get ready to leave Earth Mother who give him birth. He gonna get ready to fly free over lands."

"What happens when he's free?"

Now it was her turn to grin. "That be lesson stuff for tomorrow."

"Then it'll be *good* for a change?"

"Yup. But now we talk 'bout stuff that happen when he crouch, getting ready to fly free. This be time when many stuff gonna stop."

"Then this is a good lesson too," I said expectantly.

"Nope."

Sigh.

"This be when bad stuff gonna stop all right." She raised a cautioning finger. "But *bad* stuff gonna stop bad stuff. See?"

I didn't.

"Listen Summer, remember last week we speak 'bout bad stuff state gonna do? Now, now when Phoenix be crouched, peoples gonna turn stuff 'round. They be plenty angry at state. They fight back."

"Rioting?"

"That be later. First they not pay monies to state."

"People will refuse to pay their taxes?"

"Yup. They be tired of paying so many monies. They not pay more until laws change."

I thought about this. I thought about people I've read about who cheated on their tax returns, or worse yet, refused to pay them entirely. The consequences weren't worth the personal rebellion. I thought of the commotion that a mass taxation refusal would create. "I don't think everyone would do this, No-Eyes. Most people want to do things right—within the law."

"Even when state take too much?"

"Yes, even then. People don't want to risk getting into trouble."

"They gonna. Summer not have to be one."

"I don't think I could. I don't like upsetting the apple cart."

"What this apple cart be?"

"Just another way of saying going against things."

"Apple cart gonna spill over on side. It be one big mess even. But tax stuff only be one stuff peoples gonna stop doing. They not like state taking sons to war. Peoples gonna hide sons away. Sons gonna run to other countries even."

"That's called draft evasion," I clarified.

"No-Eyes not care what it be called."

"Okay, but if that's going to happen, then they'll reinstate the draft, right now it's not in effect."

"State gonna do that for sure. State need more sons to fight wars, wars that be no wars even."

"And the people will resist by sending their sons away or moving the entire family to a different country."

"That right. Some families not gonna move. They only stay to fight state 'bout this."

"No-Eyes, those sons will simply be put in jail if they refuse to fight."

She thought before she answered. "Some maybe, but there be too many. This law be only tiny part of stuff here. Peoples not gonna like wars that be no wars. See? They gonna fight state 'bout wars. Peoples get plenty angry, they fight back!"

I still didn't see how the general masses could effectively accomplish all these resistances. "I still don't see."

"What to see? Peoples no like wars, taxes. They gonna sit down, refuse. Too many be together for state to make people do stuff see?"

"I guess I'll have to. What happens now, when so many people refuse?"

A twinkle lit her eye. "That what be most important stuff here, Summer. That what be good stuff."

I was glad to be finally getting around to this good stuff of hers.

"State peoples see how strong people be. They see how strong peoples feel 'bout war stuff, tax stuff. State peoples be confused, they fight together."

"This isn't clear. Who fights together? The people against the state?"

She slapped her knee over the irony of it. "No! State peoples gonna fight state peoples. See Summer, state peoples be mixed up! They not agree no more on law stuff. It gonna be big fight!"

"That's definitely clear. The government will see that their laws aren't working, that the people won't stand for tax exploitation or the forced induction of their sons into wars they don't believe in, and the government will disagree on the validity of its own laws and policies. The goverment will have its own inner revolt."

She cackled until her pink gums showed. "That right. That how it gonna be!"

As I thought about the prospect I worried.

She frowned. "What the matter?"

I shrugged. "I don't like revolts. There's always bloodshed. Isn't there any other way to change the policies of the government?"

"Blah! Peoples gonna finally win! That be good thing, huh, Summer."

Silence.

"Summer?"

"What," I replied in a low disgusted tone.

"It gonna be okay. It not gonna be so bad," she consoled.

It was *all* bad. Sure, it was good that bad laws were going to be changed. It was good that bad policies were going to be reversed. It was good that young men wouldn't be forced into going to senseless wars that weren't even declared wars, but I didn't agree with the method that was going to be utilized to bring about these positive changes. I couldn't justify the means and I said as much to her.

She maintained her staunch disagreement. "Some stuff gonna happen anyway. Summer not have any say."

I tried another alternate. "What if another leader was in the government, would that probability prevent any of this?"

"Nope. Leader not be only person to make laws. Leader got many peoples who give advice, make laws. See?"

"But wouldn't a change in those advisors create a different outcome?"

Creak-thud. Creak-thud.

"Well wouldn't it?" I demanded.

"It already be in future. Summer try to change stuff here. Stuff gonna come anyway."

I was mentally scrounging around for possible avenues out of the foreseen resistance and subsequent rioting revolts. "What about the law of probabilities then? Huh, No-Eyes? What about that?" I barked defensively.

She shook her head at my continued stubborness. "Summer got head in ground here. That law only gonna put stuff off." Creak-thud. "Stuff gonna come anyways."

And suddenly I didn't care about the beautiful day. I was again plunged into the dark reality of the world's erring ways and the unavoidable havoc those ways would reap.

Flying Free

And with a massive wingspan,
the phoenix lifted himself high into
the air, soaring higher and higher
he lifted the veil of ignorance and
brought freedom to the oppressed,
truth to all humanity.

Saturday night, some friends stopped by. They were aware intellectuals in the fields of higher education and engineering. Their interest in my lessons were intensified by their present subject matter. The seven of us sat around the living room. We were concerned as we discussed the material in depth. The fascinating subject with its endless ramifications swept us into the early morning hours.

Sunday I awoke to ominously dark skies and I hoped that Mother Nature wasn't presenting me with a bad omen for my last lesson of the Phoenix manifest. My deep anxiety woke me earlier than usual, everyone was still sound asleep.

As I brushed my hair in the bathroom, Rainbow sleepily meandered around the doorway with her tail wagging. The family nearly loved her to death. She had all her needs taken care of and she never had to worry about the ugly future. She lived from one minute to the next without a care or concern. I wrapped my arms around her and hugged firmly. She planted several moist kisses on my chin and sauntered back to the softness of the girls' bed. And I wished life could be so simple for people.

When I went outside, a sharp chill crossed my face. It looked and felt like it was getting ready to snow but I knew that it wouldn't—not yet. I had the roads to myself and as I turned up the heater, I imagined the warmth that would be permeating through my teacher's cabin. She would be rocking by the fireplace, waiting patiently for her student to arrive. I could clearly hear the familiar creak and thud of the wobbly chair. Her bright eyes would be firmly fixed upon the dancing flames. She would be mentally getting her lesson plan ready.

I too needed to be prepared for my last lesson. I was greatly relieved that this day was going to be the final phase of the future talks. Although she had said that the last one was going to be good news, I held reservations about that aspect. Yet, in my own heart, I wanted to believe that the worst was over now that the great Phoenix was going to be flying free.

Just as I had imagined, the snaking trail of smoke rising from her stone chimney gave evidence of the blazing fire that was warming my classroom. It was a comforting sight and I wasted no time reaching it.

Again, I disobediently flung her door open.

In a flash, the old woman turned in her chair and opened her mouth to bark at me. "*Summer....*"

"I know, I know," I immediately interrupted, "I'm gonna break your door yet. But see," I said softly as I gently closed it, "see how quietly I can close it?"

She clucked her tongue, grinned and faced the fire again. "Summer *scare* No-Eyes. No-Eyes think that door gonna break for sure this time."

I removed my serape and went to her chair. "That's a new one. Think of all the lesson times when you got *me* so scared. It doesn't feel very good, does it," I teased playfully.

She shook a boney finger at me. "Summer think No-Eyes not ever be scared too when we have those important lessons? No-Eyes not be too sure Summer gonna do okay, not too sure Summer gonna make right decisions. *That* scare No-Eyes *plenty!*"

I was truly surprised at her revelation. "Why you little sneak! You never let on that you were scared too. You always appeared so calm and collected."

Her shoulders hitched up and then fell. "Teacher not s'posed to let on that she be scared too. That not be sign of good teacher. See?"

I shook my head from side to side and patted her hand. "So that's it. But why admit it now?"

"What so! Summer know lot more stuff now. We know each other complete now. We be like one person here." And she grinned wide.

"No-Eyes, we've been like one person for a long time now."

The grin was suddenly gone. She reached over and placed her other hand over mine and squeezed. "Summer, even when I be gone . . . we still gonna be like one peoples."

Seriousness smothered our playful mood like a wet blanket thrown over a smoldering fire. I didn't like the new direction she was leading our light bantering into. She was making it heavy. "You'll always be in my heart, No-Eyes, no matter where you are."

The medicine woman stared hard into my eyes. "And I gonna always be with Summer."

The fire wildly flickered. It danced feverishly before us as we watched in silence. And it was then that the full meaning of her words grabbed at my heart. That one sentence would mean more to me in times to come than anything else that had ever come from her lips, for after her physical presence was finally taken away from me, her spirit would join me in the wee hours of the morning as I wrote these books and she'd help me recreate our lesson days—our exact conversations. And I knew then that I'd never really ever lose my dear old friend.

"What Summer be thinking 'bout?" she asked softly.

My heart was full of a new comfort that warmed it. "That you'll really never leave me after all."

She grinned with sparkling eyes. "We only gonna be a veil away."

"And we can part that veil, huh No-Eyes."

"Yup, we gonna do that all right," she confirmed impishly.

Creak-thud. Creak-thud. And the rocker sounded the gavel that announced a change of subject matter.

I stretched out on my back with my arms folded behind my head. The fire felt homey and I was in a good position to see my teacher's face as she spoke. I waited.

Looking out at the grey sky, then back to the fire, she began the lecture. "Great Phoenix gonna be leaving torn birthland now. He spread great wings wide, crouch low and take off in first long flight through sky. Phoenix gonna fly high over all lands. He gonna glide and bring truth, freedom to all peoples who be left."

"Left. Does that mean that the horrible events will finally be over?" I inquired hopefully.

"Summer be assuming here?"

"No, not at all. I'm asking."

Creak-thud.

Waiting.

"Yup, pretty much." Then, "Yup, they be all over."

Relief. Maybe this *was* going to be the good lesson I'd been anxiously waiting to hear. "No more freak accidents? No more natural disasters, rioting crowds or unexpected bombs?"

"That be right. No more bad stuff here now."

I rolled over on my side so I could look directly into the fire occasionally. I had a lot of questions. "No-Eyes, will there be any government left?"

"Yup. It be good one. It gonna be one for *all* peoples." She didn't offer more. She was expecting the student to think out the lesson by asking the questions, then she would fill in anything I left out.

"Then the peoples' revolts and resistances will succeed in bringing about the desired changes."

She merely nodded.

I searched her face. "What'll cause the earth to suddenly settle?"

Silence.

I was going to have to figure that one out on my own. And it became clear as I thought about what had caused it to become angered in the first place. "The peace of men will settle the earth."

She granted me her affirmation. "Yup. Men get so bad they make Earth Mother shake, boil, and explode even. Then men be good, they be peaceful, have good vibrations again. Earth Mother gonna like that, she settle back down, be peaceful. Besides, Phoenix be out flying free then."

"Yeah, he's flying over us then. He'll bring peaceful times for those who are left."

We were both silent. I thought of more questions while she patiently waited for them. "No-Eyes, you mentioned the other day that the Indian nation would be strong again. I don't really understand how that can become an actuality, and I can't seem to come up with the right questions for it. Can you help me out with this one?"

"Yup."

I waited for more than one word.

Creak-thud. "Think!"

I tried. I thought out loud. "Well, if the peoples' resistance wins and the government realizes its errors in policies," I paused out of uncertainty, "and the new government is good for the people; then I guess everyone will be equal, there won't *be* any more minority races."

Creak-thud. "And?" she urged.

That's as far as I could get. "And that's all I can think of," I admitted sheepishly knowing what her reply would be.

"Blah! Summer do better, go farther than *that!* Think *more!*"

"I flattened out on my stomach and set my chin down on my hands. The fire was almost too warm on my face, but I ignored it as I thought deeper into the problem. When it dawned on me, I was mortified to admit to my shallow thinking. Then my eyes lit up with a new realization and I quickly turned back on my side again. As I did, the woman's eyes twinkled with pride. "See? Summer not be so dumb. Go on, tell No-Eyes why Indian nation gonna rise again."

I was beaming. "Because the peaceful people are going to be aware! They're going to see that the Indians believed and lived the right way all along—the Earthway. They're going to seek them out to learn more from them. Right?"

Her pink gums said it all. "That be right. Peoples gonna first see that Blacks, Asians and Hispanics be just as good as white peoples. Peoples gonna then see that women be just as good as men even. *All* peoples gonna be equal, be like brothers—be *one* peoples."

My heart skipped a beat. "You didn't mention the Indian race."

Creak-thud. Creak-thud.

I raised up on one elbow. "No-Eyes, aren't the Indians going to be equal, one with everyone too?"

Silence.

It was thinking time again. "Well, if the Indians aren't equal and there aren't anymore minority races, then...then I still don't get it because you said that nobody would be superier either."

She leaned forward. "Summer be right. There not *gonna* be any superior races when Phoenix be flying free."

I was frustrated with my dead end.

She leaned back. "We go see. Bring up spirit."

I was anxious to get to the bottom of this perplexing mystery. I sighed and lay down again. The fire crackled in my ear and the shadows flickered across my darkened eyelids. My heart pounded as I worked to consciously slow the racing beat before I could accomplish any further steps.

I concentrated on the fire sensations. I allowed the warmth to spread a calm wave over my body. The snapping logs sent out homey visions and I received the peacefulness into my being. My arms relaxed and my spine sunk down on the braided rug. The physical tension was lifting. The heart rate slowed and I began to take shallow breaths. I saw the bright flames before my eyes and I mentally moved them up to my forehead where they flickered and licked to reach upward until I was finally free. I took my waiting teacher's outstretched hand.

"That not take too long. We gonna go see now."

We drifted a short while until we were again in the Corridor of Time. Beings were purposefully moving to and fro through the massive etheric tunnel.

No-eyes winked at me. "Summer feel better here now?"

"Yeah, I'm not afraid anymore."

She smiled. "Not have stuff to be afraid of in first place."

"Well," I defended, "now I know where I am."

She shrugged. "Many places maybe scare Summer. Places not have to do that scare stuff. Summer relax. Summer be aware and not be scared, that all. It be simple."

"Yeah, that's just all there is to it," I replied sarcastically.

She sighed at her bad student's attitude. "Anyways, we gonna go see stuff Summer no can figure out."

We moved effortlessly through the busy spirit byway. I saw excited beings, beings who were obviously intently preoccupied with their own special missions, and beings who were saddened.

I watched several of them take the time to offer consolation with their unique sympathetic love meld. And all I saw gave my spirit reason to rejoice. I witnessed the truth to life, the living proof of the spirit's ongoing reality.

Then, I suddenly realized that my knowledgeable companion wasn't beside me. I was alone. I frantically whirled around and felt immediate relief when I spotted her standing twenty paces behind me. I rushed back to her side.

"Where Summer think she be going?" she humorously admonished.

"I'm sorry. I got so taken up with all of these . . . "

"Summer go too far in future." She pointed to the wavering wall. "This be where we gonna get off." And she disappeared through the nebulous material of the tunnel.

I hastily followed and found her already beginning to descend through the warming atmosphere of the future earth.

I quickly caught up. "You *wait* for me!" I snapped breathlessly.

She ignored my rudeness and suddenly stopped cold. She was intently listening.

I followed suit.

The earth appeared to be pulsating. It was a gentle and steady sort of rhythm. I strained to distinguish what was making the muted throbbing sound. And, turning to No-Eyes, I gave her a confounded look.

She placed a finger to her lips and led me slowly downward. The persistent beat remained constant. I was expecting it to gain in intensity as we neared the earth, but it continued to palpitate at the same soft decible—an almost inaudible rate of vibration.

We descended upon a sun-touched western plain that was literally teaming with grazing cattle. Their combined lowing was humorous. I looked to my friend for an explanation of the common scene. "What's so unusual about this?"

"Summer better take longer look," she instructed.

I returned my gaze to the four-footed people. And after watching them for a short time, I realized what made them so unusual. "There's entire *families* of cattle here! *Look*, No-Eyes! Look at those *old* ones!" I was so completely taken up with the amazing scene, it was like *I* was the one showing *her* something new.

She was smiling.

I couldn't get over it. I actually found it difficult to believe my own eyes, and my heart leapt with joy while I moved in closer to the animals. I looked deeply into their large brown eyes and realized that they'd never be heartlessly led to the slaughterhouse—they'd never be *eaten*! and I felt like crying as I attempted to touch the soft downy fur on a calf's head. It sensed my presence and romped off to it's mother's side for safety. I looked back at my teacher.

She was motioning for me to look in another direction.

And when I followed her finger, I saw hundreds and hundreds of acres of wheat that wavered gently in the wind. Then she pointed to more acres that grew healthy tall corn. In another direction, alfalfa was growing. It was so beautiful.

The wheat made hushing sounds as the breeze softly swished it from side to side. The corn rustled as it too sang its joyous giving song, and the alfalfa merely whispered as the tender fingers of the wind plucked upon its deep green strands.

I wanted to listen forever to this hallowed symphony of earthly peace, but my teacher was only beginning. I was led elsewhere.

"We gonna see building stuff now," she said lightheartedly as we drifted into a residential area.

New sounds came to me, harsher sounds. Men were laughing and humming as they busily hammered and nailed and sawed on the new houses. The sounds were different from the construction noises I was used to hearing. And the sight of the product of their effort was most unusual.

The men were constructing houses that didn't look like houses at all. They were circular. They were partially underground and utilized the sun for their only source of power. Then I realized why the construction sounds were different—I didn't hear any of the usual deafening power tools. The men were manually sawing and nailing!

My teacher spoke. "Plenty stuff gonna be different in future."

I was truly amazed. "But the houses, they're all in the earth!"

She smiled warmly. "Yup, they be like Earth Mother. Earth Mother like them there. She like being one to hold people.

Upon closer inspection, I made observations about the houses new configurations. "They're *circular.*"

"Yup. They be round to keep unity of energy within."

I was so happy that I must've looked like a real idiot standing there grinning from ear to ear.

She pulled on my arm. "We not be done yet."

I followed her to a church of some kind. It was outside in an open area. People were seated on the ground. They had their legs crossed. Suddenly, they rose in unison and raised their arms to the blue sky and gave thanks. They thanked God for the rich earth. They gave thanks for their flowing waters and the warm sun. And they thanked God for each other, their brothers. There didn't appear to be a leader who conducted the ceremonies. They acted as one unit.

I turned to No-Eyes for an explanation.

"They not need leader here. They know what they be thankful for. They pray, that all that be needed. We gonna go back now. No-Eyes think Summer got good 'nough idea now."

And I did.

We drifted away from the earth and paused high in space.

I whispered to my teacher. "Why didn't we simply return to the cabin?"

"Shh, look." She pointed down to the rotating planet.

I peered down and saw a world at peace. The beautiful orb slowly rotated beneath a veil of whispy white clouds. It was so magnificently restful. I wanted to cry, but what really brought on my tears was the rosy aura that pulsated from the earth—it was the aura of absolute love.

"Now Summer think 'bout cabin." And she vanished.

I hovered above the homey cabin room. I loved this room. I watched the fire choreograph a frenzied mazurka that threw the shadows prancing and kicking gaily about the room. The darkened smoke-damaged walls were literally alive with the staccato reflections of the fire's dizzying folkdance.

I inhaled deeply of the woodsmoke while the heady incense of piñon and juniper wafted near my ceiling vantage point. And in the broken rocking chair, sat my old friend. I drifted near her and saw her watching over my resting form. She knew that I had returned, but was respecting my spirit's melancholy moment. I paused a second, then reentered.

My eyes fluttered. I stretched. I ached from the hardness of the pine floor that had made itself evident through the thin worn rug.

"Summer better get back up on couch," she thoughtfully advised.

I smiled and readily took her suggestion. When I was settled, and after she faced her chair to me, I had a nagging question. "What was that pulsing sound we heard when we first saw the earth?"

"No-Eyes gonna get to that. First, what Summer think of future world?"

I stared into the glowing embers. "It was beautiful, so very, very beautiful."

"Yup. It gonna be that all right."

My mind was swirling with the beauty. "There were so many positive reversals. I'm not sure which one I'm more excited about." I gave them deeper thought. "The new style of housing will mean a great deal to the people. They will bring the people into a closer relationship with the earth and the new configuration will retain the people's energies. The endless fields of grain were simply beautiful, but I think I'm most excited about the four-leggeds—they'll finally be free. Their spared lives are what I liked the best. Not only for the creatures themselves, but also for the people who'll be so much better off—healthier."

"But Summer not get to see *all* animals there. There be woods full of deer families too, rabbit and elk families. There be prairies full of buffalo families roaming free too!"

"Oh God, will it really come to that?"

"Summer see with own eyes. It not be only words here. Summer *saw*!"

"Yeah, I did didn't I."

Creak-thud. Creak-thud.

My racing mind was reviewing the film again. "And those houses! They reminded me of. . . . "

Creak-thud.

"*Indian* homes. They were *always* circular." The light was dawning. "And the men's *manual* use of tools, and the *prayers! No-Eyes*!"

"Yup, that be how Indian peoples gonna fit in stuff. That be how Indian nation gonna rise strong again. All peoples gonna go back, gonna live like Indian. They take spirit ways of Indian. They gonna live in peace with all life, with Earth Mother, just like Indian gonna show them to—how to live Earthway."

I rested back against the couch and felt a gentle wave of tranquility wash over me. Then I realized that my wise friend still hadn't answered my initial question yet. "Is it time to talk about my question yet?"

"What question be that?"

"You know, that rhythmic pulsation sound I heard."

She spread her hands on her lap and raised her whispy brows high over wide owl eyes. "Summer not know what that be?" she asked in animated amazement.

I shook my head guiltily.

Creak-thud. Creak-thud.

"I suppose I should know, huh." I bit my lip. "But honestly I don't. Care to give me a hint?"

The rocker became silent. The old woman leaned far forward, bringing her face into the dancing firelight that reflected her new radiating joy. "Summer, that be rhythm of great new universal hearbeat. That heartbeat be throbbing of freedom drums that just *now* beginning." She stretched closer, tenderly placing a brown hand upon my knee. "Listen Summer, listen and hear the soft shufflings of thousands of anxious moccasins. They be moving restless upon the Earth Mother—even now. That pulse sound be beginning drums of future, *now*."

I was about to speak when she raised a cautioning finger and whispered, "Summer, be still. Listen." She suspensefully cocked her head. "Listen to faint drumbeat that be carried on the wind. Shh... hear it?"

I attempted to calm my thundering heart. The forceful wind was gathering momentum outside my quiet classroom. It boldly knocked on the door and rapped hard on the windowpanes. Yet, underneath the wind's boisterous commotion, I detected the steady meter of a nebulous sound. I bent down to place my palms on the warm pine floor and I felt the distinct vibration of the earth's heartbeat, the decisive rhythm of its own strong drums. My heart raced like a wild horse across his golden canyon and I grinned. I smiled up at my teacher who was beaming with the knowledge of the earth's rarely shared secrets.

"Summer can feel it, huh."

Leaning back against the pillows, I felt like I was just made aware of a very secret and mystical fact. "But surely we two aren't the *only* people who sense this," I commented softly.

Creak-thud.

What was that supposed to mean? I tried again. "There are a lot of aware people in the world, No-Eyes. Why haven't *they* spoken up about the beautiful pulsing?"

"Humph."

Silence. Thinking.

"Well... I realize that certain Indians, the wise ones who kept the old ways close to their hearts, are aware of it. Yet, there must also be people of other races who are aware enough to detect it."

The dilapidated rocker made a split-second pause, then regained its former voice. I must've struck a chord of truth in something I had said. I thought deeper.

A sudden tongue-clicking broke my deep reverie. "Tsk-tsk. Summer not ever gonna come to right thought here 'cause I not ever *tell* reason why peoples not speak of drumbeat vibration of earth."

There she goes again, expecting me to come to a realization when I had no factual information to derive it from. She was playfully toying with me like a frisky kitten with a new ball of yarn. "Are you going to tell me or are you just going to leave me dangling in my ignorance?"

"I no dangle Summer."

"Good." I interrupted the conversation to stoke the embers and add several twisted piñon logs. "Let's move closer to the fire, all right?"

She nodded agreeably and dragged the chair around to face the fire that crackled and sparked with renewed vigor.

I swiped a couple of the lumpy pillows from the couch, tossed them on the floor and punched them into a comfortable position against the rough fireplace stones.

"Gonna beat up No-Eyes' pillows!" she barked.

I laughed. "No I'm not. I'm gonna beat down the lumps. They're already pretty well beaten up. Anyway, I like them this way." I sunk down into the cushions and stared into the friendly fire. Then I turned to my old friend and watched the flames flutter their orange reflections over her deeply wrinkled face.

"What Summer see?" she whispered with a tone of calculating wisdom.

Her probing question brought on a deeply solemn mood. "Wisdom. Love. A special friend."

The dry corners of her mouth lifted ever so perceptively, then relaxed. "What else?"

I rested my chin on my knees. I didn't answer her immediately because I wasn't sure what she was fishing for. "I'm not sure, No-Eyes. I'm really not sure. Sometimes when I review our first meeting, how strange it was, and then the way we've spent so many instruction days together, I try to attach some sane semblance of logic to it. It's incredible, the entire scenario is just so unreal at times, it's so . . . . "

"What Summer see?" she repeated softly. The rocker remained still—she was intense now, yet she spoke with a loving gentleness.

I searched her dark eyes. "I see an Indian woman."

The ebony, saucerlike eyes were bottomless pools that shimmered with an undulating essence of silvery mercury. Their depths bored through mine. "No-Eyes see Indian woman too."

Her unexpected words had released a powerful lance that came hurdling through the air to plunge deep into my heart. I reclined on my side from the impact and I stared at the massive rafters while I attempted to ease the sudden pain. I was hurting inside.

Creak-thud.

Silence. Bleeding inside.

"Summer not believe what No-Eyes see?"

Silence.

"Well?"

I snuck a quick glance up at her, then I studied the wavering forms on the ceiling. When I spoke, my voice cracked with uncertainty. "It's not that I don't believe what you see, it's just not quite the same, that's all."

The old one bent forward. "Why it not same? Summer look at No-Eyes and see Indian woman. No-Eyes look at Summer and see Indian woman too. What so?" She knew what torment wracked my heart and was attempting to perform a healing on it.

I remained mute.

She rested back into the rocker, closed her eyes and wisely waited for her patient to describe the symptoms.

My next painful words were barely audible. "I still think I'm the wrong one, No-Eyes."

Again she tilted her chair forward, drawing her face down nearer to mine. "Wrong one? There not be *wrong* stuff here, Summer. *All* stuff go down just like it *meant* to."

I retained the aching doubt. "Maybe, maybe not," I whispered softly.

She cocked her heard to one side, allowing the firelight to light up the whispy hairs that had come loose around her face, framing it in a silvery aura. She spoke with gentle authority. "*No* mistakes be *tolerated* here. Summer cannot back out. There not be some magic back door that Summer can slip out of. All stuff meant to be. *Summer* be woman who *meant* here."

I locked my eyes firmly on hers. "I'm not actually attempting to back out. I. . .I just don't think this carryover soul concept will make it yet, it's too new, people won't understand.

"No-Eyes. . .even *I* have a hard time dealing with it. I feel so. . .so mismatched. I feel like some freak trying to fit in with the mainstream of life." A hard lump was beginning to form somewhere deep within my chest. I attempted to ignore it. "My heart, my spirit, my memory is totally Indian, and yet, where is my Indian nation? I look at the world and everything in it through the eyes of an Indian." My gaze quickly searched the ceiling in a feeble attempt to contain the sudden flooding in them. "I. . .I think like an old, old Indian yet. . . ."

"Now why Summer be crying?" she asked sympathetically.

Silence.

Creak-thud.

Blinking back the tears, I gained a small measure of composure. "I think I'm the wrong one. A fullblood should've been led into your woods that day—not me. Sometimes I lay in bed at night and I think 'why me?' "

A flash of understanding illuminated the old woman's face. "Summer think she not be worthy for job here?"

"I don't know for sure. I guess I just feel that something isn't falling completely into place. And I feel that I'm the odd puzzle piece that stands alone. Don't you see?"

"Blah!"

"That's no answer. You're copping out on me."

"Nope. That be No-Eyes' answer to dumb statement, that all."

"It wasn't dumb."

"Was dumb. It be dumb, dumb, dumb. Summer, Indian nation now full of soft Indians. They get deep into white ways, they forget old sacred ways, beliefs. They not want to remember how to make weather change in blink of eye, they not have interest in hard work it take to learn and keep sacred stuff strong in hearts.

"True, there be some special ones who keep sacred stuff alive, but they hurt bad inside 'cause they be so few, 'cause so few young ones want to bother with the hard efforts it take to learn stuff. That gonna change though. Summer gonna bring back heritage ways. Summer gonna make Indian hearts puff with new pride, new meaning to heritage. Summer be Spirit Woman."

Silence. Doubting.

"Summer, listen. All this stuff be written long ago." She waved her arms through the air. "Oh, it not be written down on any paper, 'cause that not be Indian way. It be written on wind. It be ancient knowledge that be whispered by mountains. The trees know 'bout it. The four-leggeds know 'bout it. Wise people who take time to listen know 'bout it too. All truths be universal in all of nature, we not need written words to learn truth. We learn of truth from its source, and that be nature!

"Some people cannot pick, cannot choose in life. Some people have to follow own path, path that feel right in heart and in spirit. All peoples be here to do best stuff they meant to do. Summer suffer many years searching down her own right path. Summer go this way, and go that way, but she find right end of line all the same. End of line not always be what people expect. Summer find end of line in No-Eyes' forest out there. No-Eyes not ever be tricked. No coyote ever been able to fool old No-Eyes. I know who you be first time I set my mind eyes on you. No Summer, no mistakes made here. Summer not come in coyote skin. Beside, listen to me, fullblood no good for this job."

That last mysterious statement made no logical sense at all.

"What is that supposed to mean?"

She tenderly gave a knowing smile. "Well...No-Eyes just gonna get to that stuff. Summer live many, many years as fullblood Shoshoni. Summer cannot help that her Indian memory, mind, heart and spirit still be that same Indian woman's. But what be most important here, is that Summer now fullfill old Indian prophesy." She grinned wide with the secret I knew nothing about.

I was watchful. I felt she was merely trying to make me feel better. "No jokes, No-Eyes, I'm not in the mood." I rolled over onto my stomach and thoughtfully picked at the frayed threads of the worn braided rug.

She was outwardly infuriated by my unbelieving attitude. She stamped her foot. "I *not* make joke here! This not be *joke* time. This be damn serious *stuff!*"

I shot a hard look at her. She wasn't grinning anymore and she had sworn for the first time on top of it. I was genuinely shocked. "You *swore!*"

She shrugged. "That only be way to emphasize words. Right?"

I snickered. "Right."

A thin finger came snaking toward me. "But Summer not gonna make No-Eyes swear again. Summer gonna stop this sorry feeling stuff and listen good!"

Her manner was half anger and half sympathy. She knew precisely how I had been feeling and was going to repair the damage I had done to myself. "Now," she began authoritatively, "No-Eyes speak 'bout that prophesy stuff. I not mumble here. I not be some senile old woman."

I grinned.

"This not be funny stuff either. This be serious!"

I wiped the grin off and prepared to listen to her serious stuff.

"Now, Summer be right 'bout peoples of other races who sense stuff. But they not tell 'cause it not be right time, they waiting.

"Summer also be right 'bout some wise Indians who know stuff too. But they keep stuff up here," pointing to her forehead, "and in here," pounding her thin chest. "They keep plenty serious stuff just between them...."

"How come I never heard of this old prophecy?"

"How come Summer be led here to learn?"

I felt resigned and duly admonished. "And I still am learning, aren't I."

Creak-thud.

Silence.

The snapping fire choreographed a frenzied dance of shadows

over the log walls. The nodding flames warmed my tired body, and No-Eyes' words glowed within my spirit. I thought on her words. Perhaps I didn't have a personal stronghold over my final destiny. Perhaps I never did. Things ultimately hadn't worked out as I had always envisioned them. And, according to my wise teacher, we can't compose our own songs or write our own life's endings. We merely march to the individual tune or follow the path that fate has penned for us. Consequently, our final destination often turns out to be something far different than what we were expecting, planning, or searching for. This particular thought made me remember a dream I had experienced the previous night and I let my mind dwell on it while No-Eyes quietly rocked deep within her own solitude.

"Summer think No-Eyes take nap here?"

Her sudden voice startled me. "You did look like you were beginning to doze off."

"Nope. Summer gonna tell No-Eyes 'bout that dream."

It had been a strange dream, yet it was so very real. I hadn't planned on sharing it with my friend, but since she inquired about it, and since it wouldn't do any good for me to refuse, I gave in quickly. "You've been in my head again," I casually chastised.

"Yup," she freely admitted without reserve, "and it be good thing too. That dream be big message for dreamer. Maybe dreamer not know that yet. Dream say important stuff. Summer tell now."

I sat up with my arms wrapped around my knees. Perhaps subconsciously, I had been wishing all along that she'd ask to hear it. Perhaps I needed her interpretation to put my doubts at rest once and for all.

And I began the telling.

"It was night. The moon was a huge silver disc that hung in the bitter sky. I knelt and began digging with my bare hands into the snow-covered earth. I was digging where someone called Weaver Woman told me to dig. I was very anxious to discover what I was supposed to find. Someone was on their knees next to me watching me dig. This person was also anxious to see what I would find.

"Suddenly, my long hair became frozen to the ground within the hole that I had excavated. I pulled back in an effort to free my hair, but something was firmly attached to it from within the dark hole. I was repulsed to see that it was a medicine rattle made from a human hairball. I thought it was from the person whose grave I was digging in. I was terribly frightened by this thing that was frozen to the ends of my hair. I screamed for the person next to me to pull it off. This person was paralyzed with a dreaded horror and finally ran from me. And then, without touching the hairball, I tried to swat it off by swinging my hair and whacking the rattle several times against a bright gaslight pole—the pole merely slightly dented.

"Then I entered a familiar house. I was cradling the rattle in my hands trying to hide it until I found who I was looking for. I spotted Weaver Woman reading a newspaper and I secretly bent over to show her what was attached to my hair. Her eyes lit up at the sight of the sacred object and she carefully reached out for it. It gently fell away from my hair and into her hands when she touched it. She then did an amazing thing. She appeared to unravel the hairball medicine rattle. It rolled out between her delicate hands. It rolled out to transform into a scroll-like papyrus. The beautifully scribed design was fastened between two sticks and had a combination of Egyptian hieroglyphics and Indian petroglyphs on it. 'This is the Spirit Woman's Sacred Medicine Sheild and now it is rightfully yours,' she softly said while handing it back to me.

"Suddenly, it was a brilliant sunny morning. I was standing on a grassy hill with the papyrus in my hands. I stood under a massive tree. Weaver Woman walked toward me. She had an armful of silver bars with a beautiful piece of blue stone resting on top. 'These are yours,' she said holding them out to me, 'if you would've dug deeper in that hole, you would've found them.' Then I saw a great circle of clouds rotating above us. They slowly descended down from the sky."

I anxiously waited for No-Eyes to comment on the dream.

Silence.

"Well? What do you think?" I asked anxiously.

"It not be what No-Eyes think that count here. What Summer think?"

"I think that Weaver Woman represented the Storyteller—the person who keeps the Truth alive, in other words, the Spirit of the Truth." I looked to my teacher for confirmation.

None came.

I continued with my interpretation. "I dug in the night, which represents mystery or an unknown or hidden knowledge." Again I glanced quickly up at my silent mentor. Then, after seeing that she wanted me to go on, I did. "The snow covering the earth meant truth just below the surface, truth long frozen in time. The grave meant a people or a way of life long buried. The person next to me represented mankind who is also anxious to seek the truth. My hair represented my thoughts and they became suddenly, firmly connected to . . . to you, No-Eyes. The medicine rattle was *you* bringing the ancient wisdom up out of the buried past and into my thoughts, my mind."

She stirred. Bending low, she asked, "If this hairball medicine rattle represent No-Eyes, then why Summer been so repulsed by it?"

I thought about that inconsistency. "Because I was afraid of touching the sacred truth. I felt unfit."

She rested peacefully back into the chair that began a gentle rocking. "Go on, Summer."

"Well...then this other person was horrified to see me with the sacred truths."

She interrupted. "Many peoples not recognize truth no matter who have it. They in shock to see somebody with real truth. Real truth represent great powers."

I nodded. "But why did I try to get the rattle off by knocking it against that pole?"

"Summer not want to touch it. Remember little while ago Summer say she not think she be the right one? Summer not want to be the one who bring truth out into sunlight? In dream, Summer try to give truth back to truth, gaslight represent that eternal light—truth."

I thought how good she was with her interpretation, then I finished the dream out. "I guess I wasn't afraid of it anymore because when I was in that house where others were, I wanted to protect the rattle so I cradled it until I found the Spirit of Truth who was Weaver Woman. And truth unraveled my rattle, my connection with you, to show me that I was strongly protected. The following day, truth brought me riches; not gold, which would signify monetary riches; but silver, which meant spiritual riches. And the massive tree I stood under indicated the sacred Tree of Heritage and the circle of clouds meant the return of unity descending upon the earth."

"Not exactly," came her comment. "Summer got all symbols right 'cept this cloud circle stuff. Listen. Those clouds mean great Hoop gonna come whole again, be strong 'round Tree, Great Hoop of Nations gonna descend and be strong again."

Silence.

"Summer remember 'bout Hoop of Nations and Sacred Tree?"

"Of course, everybody knows about those."

"Not everybody, Summer."

Silence.

"But everybody gonna know soon 'nough, huh."

Silence. And I contemplated on my beautiful untouchable past. I mentally experienced subliminal frames of the lost scenes of a way of life I left far behind—a time when we respected all of nature, when we thanked the four-legged spirits for their bodily gifts of sustenance, when we never failed to leave generous offerings behind to appease their spirit in our heartfelt thankfulness. I joined in the womans' circle as we chatted happily while scraping new buffalo hides. I watched my own small girl-child clumsily attempt to spiral cut a strip of white rabbit skin for her hair. And I laughed as my warrior husband playfully layed me down on soft skins in our warm lodge.

A soft whisper rent the intricate tapestry of my beautiful meditations. "Summer?"

"I'm here," I replied sorrowfully.

"It been something good. Huh, Summer."

"Yeah, something good." I stared into the leaping flames.

"But now Summer know it gonna come again. Summer have vision that come on soft wings in the skin of a dream to tell that there be no mistakes made here." She nudged my leg with her toe. "Feel the floor again. Feel the vibration of the silent drums that beat for old days return. Summer, it all gonna come back again, just like you remember it. And when the great Phoenix is flying free, look closely at what he carries lovingly within his clenched talons. It will be a new green leaf, not from an olive branch, but from the fresh growth of the Sacred Tree that will be flourishing straight and strong within the Hoop of Mankind's new Nation."

Silence.

No words were necessary anymore. No words could ever come near to matching the feeling the lump in my throat gave me.

We remained in deep contemplative stillness as we envisioned the new future. While my teacher's last eloquent words coursed through my mind, a mystical drumbeat pulsed wildly through by being. And as my heart throbbed in time with the audible thunder of the returning buffalo's hoofbeats, a lone tear fell upon the worn pine floor—the first tear of happiness that I could finally shed for mankind.

Sign of the Times— An Overview Perspective

And the Shadow of the resurrected Phoenix silently glided over all the land as a sign of man's new age of peace—peace in a universal brotherhood, peace with the Earth Mother and peace with God.

The forthcoming world changes were not a new subject for Bill and me. We had read and heard of various future prophesies that included several that my wise teacher had also foreseen. However, No-Eyes was never interested in revealing such important events in the form of broadscope generalities. She delved deeply into each future event and we discussed the consequential ramifications in detail. Confidentially, she also revealed the probable dates which I purposely deleted because, as I explained previously, pinpointing precise dates is ultimately futile because of the affectations of altering probabilities entering in. She adamantly emphasized that *no* highly enlighted individual *ever* revealed dates to the *public*, for if they did, it was a clear indication they had no comprehension of the higher concepts of universal spiritual laws governing reality. Therefore, I leave the "dated" prophesies and predictions to the Hollywood fortunetellers and prognosticators.

When my Phoenix lessons were finally concluded, Bill and I discussed them in length with several of our close friends who were knowledgeable in many of the scientific fields that the changes were to affect. We were extremely careful not to read additional material into the events. We were cautious not to alter the happenings or to make false suppositions. However, we examined each situation singly and took our judgemental considerations directly from the naked facts that our old visionary had foreseen.

The initial signs of changes, the first movements of the great Phoenix, were to be physically evidenced by major alterations in the economic structure; not only that of the U.S., but that of other nations as well.

We haven't witnessed massive strikes since before our last recession. It would appear, and logically so, that the blue collar workers are indeed grateful for any steady full-time job by which they collect regular paychecks. And the resulting financial security of those jobs naturally inhibits any motivation toward pressing a company for higher wage demands by way of strikes. When the national unemployment runs high, workers aren't inclined to bite the hand that feeds them. Yet, No-Eyes clearly foresaw the massive movement of strikes among the nation's blue collar workers. This would then indicate some type of economic upswing directly preceding the strikes. Lately, many economists have been beating their drums over the bright outlook. They reason and build their positive attitude upon the blocks of additional monies available for loans, lower interest rates, and the greater percentage of credit purchases. Yet, these economic building blocks have been here before and, just as before they are open to the probabilities for them to come tumbling down into rubble.

No-Eyes warned of surface appearances, and this positive economic growth would certainly appear to fit the bill here. It is clear that if the economy is allegedly sound, unemployment will take a temporary dive causing the workers to become secure with their sound position for bargaining leverage and then the strikes will vigorously ensue. This begins the downward trend for the grand economic slide.

Will the vehement strikers be able to win their cause? Probably not, because many of the empty factories will remain that way—filled only with the silent specters of what once was. The owners will cease their U.S. operations and take their businesses overseas where they can be assured of increased monetary profits. Major businesses and conglomerates will forsake their mother country for the hypnotic wooing of foreign soil. And the disenchanted strikers will cause a sharp rise in unemployment. The vacating companies will leave a jagged hole within the fine fabric of the stock market and Wall Street will be thrown into confusion.

During this economic melee, the far-sighted investors will quickly unload their stocks, liquidate their assets, and withdraw their funds, leaving the major banks embarrassingly overbalanced with liabilities.

With the major banks caught off guard, the people will be in a maddening rush to withdraw their assets. However, they will be gravely disappointed to discover that the F.D.I.C. has not been able to insure their hard-earned savings.

Such will be the contributing factors to the forthcoming deep recession that will hopelessly slip into depression. Money will be scarce and the remaining solvent banks will hold tightly onto their lending purses. This brings us down the spiral to the direct cause of small business failures and the sudden decline in new construction and housing starts. Small businesses will not be able to obtain their loans, construction companies will fold like a line of falling dominos and real estate will quickly devalue, all because of so little funds within the lending institutions.

We discussed the massive burden which would suddenly deluge the welfare system. It was nearly uncomprehensible. Yet it is supposed to be handled efficiently through a national food and gas rationing program, additional taxes imposed on foreign imports and an adjustment of the income tax laws which would further debilitate the remaining members of the work force by withdrawing many of their fair deductions.

As we talked about these depressing changes for our present economic way of life, we wondered about avenues that could possibly ease the future financial burdens that were sure to affect everyone.

People need to see the wisdom of making adjustments in their present-day lifestyle, their spending habits, their saving habits. We have seen that stocks will be worthless pieces of paper in the future. Long-term savings plans will only serve to tie up great blocks of assets, assets you may not ever see again.

Remember, when the time comes for these events to become a reality, you will not be able to pay for the necessities with a U.S. Savings Bond, Stock Certificate, Warranty Deed, or Credit Cards—*cash* will be the only tender accepted. Presently, some individuals believe that our society will one day be a "plastic" one. However, more and more economists are seeing evidence that this will not be so. The recent increase in credit purchasing will continue for a short time before it is realized that this method has only contributed to the ultimate economic ills that will finally befall us.

All will recognize the physical signs when the Phoenix is emerging from its birthplace.

This will be the timeframe for the natural disasters. In our fireside discussions, we agreed that the California "big one" has been overly bellowed about by tabloid psychics and doomsday sayers for years, however, that does not negate its eventual reality.

Incredible stress has been building up under the Pacific plate for many years and it is overdue to slide and release its repressed pressure. It becomes too simple to go about one's merry daily life ignoring the truth, the inevitable. People need to be made aware of the naked facts of the destructive side of nature's personality. Indeed, the stress *is* building. It is, at this very moment, inching its way to the greatest earthquake modern man has yet to be unfortunate enough to witness.

The earth is inherently unstable. It quivers and moves and builds pressure. We will experience the release of these unleashed pressures through new outlets as the earth seeks to release it any way it can. Earthquakes will be felt in areas never before reporting seismic activity. Active volcanos will violently spew forth while dormant mountain ranges and old grown-over craters will experience renewed activity.

Mt. St. Helens was a shocking surprise to everyone when it blew, even to the experienced geologists. Yet we are to witness dozens of such powerful surprises in the future.

When No-Eyes spoke of flooding during the Phoenix lessons she never brought the Great Lakes into play, but I know that she had unspokenly included them. When we had taken our psychic journey into the future to view the complete devastation of the planet, the Great Lakes were flooding down through the Mississippi River as the earth tilted into its new axis position. The land bordering the shorelines of *all* coastal regions will become inundated with a massive influx of water. Swamps will persist where arid and dry land areas once existed. And the Mississippi River will stretch its present shorelines to an incredible new width to accommodate the inrushing waters of the Great Lakes.

When the hot winds blow across the land they will wither the earth into dust bowls. They will absorb the underground springs and evaporate artesian water and create great sink holes over the land like massive moon craters. And consequently, sinking within these holes, will be large parcels of residential and city areas.

These dry winds will suck the surface moisture from the fertile lowlands and leave devastating erosion in its wake. Excessively high winds will blaze across the country, caring little for the freak deaths it leaves in its path. Tornados will increase and become the rule rather than the exception in certain areas. Hurricanes will rip into the coastal regions with increased force and destruction. Summer thunderstorms will release a ten-fold energy through intensified lightning and hail. Winters will bring frigid temperatures with its ferocious blizzards causing week-long blackouts and untolled fatalities. And when you think you perceive a greenish hue in the sky, don't wonder what it is—it's the *Phoenix Days.*

Bill and I and our friends often discussed these changes in detail, and they frequently expressed their grief over the extent the changes were going to take. One aspect that No-Eyes spoke of was totally new to us, and that was that of the great increase of transportation accidents. Of course we realized that most accidents were caused by people's unawareness, and we were continually advised of the percentage of protection that the Earth Watchers were being told to relinquish, but we never actually made the connection until No-Eyes voiced it. It is logical that people would hurt themselves more often if they were no longer being protected by unseen forces. And this was what was going to be evidenced by the massive increase of transportation accidents. It all reduced down to the common denominator of peoples' mental carelessness.

Plane crashes would occur from a mechanic's oversight during his routine maintenance checkup, or from a captain's miscalculation or from an air traffic controller's fatigue. Train derailments would occur from a switchman's error, or from a sleepy engineer or from a section of trackbed left in disrepair. Busses, automobiles, motorcycles, subways, and bicycles were all included within No-Eyes' framework of the unnecessary fatalities caused by the freak accidents. And what amazed us, was the fact that all of these disasters could be avoided if the people involved would simply take the extra time to be more aware. It was a sad and avoidable aspect of the Phoenix Days, yet because of peoples' need to hurry through their daily lives, it was to be a certain reality.

As the newborn Phoenix pauses to listen to his world, he hears tormented screams of the suffering masses.

They are hurting each other and they are injuring themselves. The increased incidents of amusement ride accidents stemming from faulty equipment didn't come as a surprise to any of us. This would be a natural companion to walk hand-in-hand with the transportation accidents caused by unawareness. But the knowledge that peoples' minds were going to crack from the pressures of the changes and be evidenced through a rash of murders and suicides was deeply depressing.

We're not advocating that you arm yourselves to the hilt, but we do suggest that extreme caution be taken. Just be more consciously aware of the careless risks that you place yourself in. Be mindful of the manner in which you handle power tools. Take the necessary safety precautions, don't cut corners when your life could very well be the

149

ultimate price paid.

The revelation of returning diseases was astonishing. It would appear that modern medicine has become complacent in its assured technology and has forgotten how to protect the masses from the age-old diseases and plagues of bygone eras.

The Bubonic Plague is transmitted through the fleas of small rodent type animals such as chipmunks, rats, squirrels, etc. These disease-ridden fleas can infest your household pets and, in turn, you. Don't be tempted to feed the cute and playful chipmunks in the park, they could very well be deadly. Protect your pets and rid your homes of rodents.

Although No-Eyes spoke mainly of the Bubonic outbreak, later, when we talked about this particular aspect of the lesson in detail, she admitted to three more diseases that would return to decimate the numbers of humanity. Two of the four epidemics clearly indicated foreign sources, not foreign in respect to originating from other countries, but foreign in respect to being the devastating products of Biological Weapons Research (germ warfare). One epidemic was seen to be directly caused by an "accidental leak" in the Utah research laboratories, and the second outbreak was seen to be an intended one.

After the Phoenix listened, he sighed and breathed heavy.

And the nations argued. They picked on and irritated one another. They falsely accused. They shouldered their blame on others and they ended up harming themselves.

The economic aspects of the Phoenix Days crossed borders and spanned the seas to affect all nations. While one country after another plummeted into depression they activated the domino theory by placing embargos on each others' imports. And the chain reaction gained in strength and momentum until it escalated into a need to step up their arms production.

Now, with each country producing more weaponry, they needed a justification for such a drastic measure. They accused and increased propaganda. Terrorism increased. They spied and stole from each other. There was no end in sight and the altercations began. It was now too late to admit that they were wrong. A government never admits to their erring ways and mistakes. And the small wars that weren't really declared wars continued. The small wars continued to claim the patriotic lives of thousands of innocent young men. Clandestine plotting and high-level secrets would be the beginning evidence of growing underhandedness utilized behind the public's back. And the general populace becomes increasingly disenchanted with the leaders they'd faithfully placed their trust it.

And the Phoenix craned his head skyward as he flexed his massive wings in an attempt to flee his warring birthland. He flexed and so did all of humanity.

This is the timeframe when the great days of questioning will occur. Certain stringent policies concerning government and education would now show up and the concept of church and state separation would seem to exist no more. And to be sure, the government would not stand idly by without countering the churches illegal invasion into its sacred domain. Certain religious sects will force their wills onto the mainstream public, more and more sects will attempt to force the return of the repressive and horrendous Age of the Inquisition. Watch for this one, for it represents a time of religious persecution—a dark, dark time of ignorance and paranoid religious suspicions.

Later, the churches will reap the effects caused by their own making, while government, in turn, interferes into their affairs. New policies are enforced concerning religious sect. Less freedoms are allowed and many non-profit exemptions and deductions are revoked while heavier taxes are imposed. And the government's retaliation is complete.

To us, the most exciting aspect of this future phase of awareness was the expected increase in space vehicle sightings. All of us, in separate incidents have physically witnessed the vehicles. And as we all now discussed the future sightings, we were filled with great excitement. No-Eyes had also included actual alien interaction with humans. This was definitely an advancement for mankind and we were anxiously looking forward to the positive results from such history-breaking achievements.

There were going to be negative reactions to this intergalactic communication. The people were going to be infuriated with the government for concealing the information. The people were going to question their religious leaders about the validity of the Creation Doctrine. There was certainly going to be a mass reevaluation. But this too was good because it would bring the people together within a united circle of the truth of the spirit. It would sow the seeds of knowledge and the thirst for truth.

This thirst will serve to awaken the mind's memory of the spirit's unique gifts, of the special senses of the spirit, and people will accept the paranormal as another clear aspect of reality. Increased efforts of learning will enhance their horizons to encompass the paranormal in elementary schools. It will be as accepted as the subjects of math and science are. And it will be a beautiful thing to see.

Also included in this will be the general acceptance of the ongoing spirit. Even though today, we have documented instances of witnessed spirit inhabitations and evidence of people leaving their physical bodies at an accident scene or during such traumatic times such as serious operations, the masses as a whole still do not accept this proven fact of reality. But when the truth is laid bare for all to view, the ultimate acceptance will be most enlightening. Yes, No-Eyes said that skeptics will forever be a part of life, but I believe that when the proof is in and the evidence is deemed undisputable, the skeptics will not then be so eager to openly admit their former beliefs.

When the great Phoenix shatters the stillness with its first wail, the nuclear times for earth will be upon us.

When I listened to my old teacher tell of these days, I cringed. I had innocently and foolishly harbored a childlike hope that the nation's illogical nuclear fetish would pass without incident. But my peaceful bubble broke with her words of discouragement. Yes, I could clearly see the present dangerous evidence of the radioactive waste dump sites and the unconscionable transportation methods of same—it was a national concern that grew stronger with each passing hour, however, to have so many sites seep its deadly contamination into densely populated areas was devastating news. I saw no viable solution to the massive problem mankind had consciously brought upon itself.

I was also naive enough to be hopeful that the near meltdowns would create such a public uproar that the remaining active nuclear plants would be shut down indefinitely. But no, mankind was not going to be intelligent enough for that final decision. After all, wouldn't that be an outright admission of error in its initial judgement? So the plants continue to operate "safely" until the ultimate meltdown, like Chernobyl, wipes out thousands of innocents with its slow-burning radiation. I can't concieve that today's advanced technology would make such a grave move in the wrong direction when there are so many clean avenues open to them. Perhaps their highly intelligent minds have advanced too far, too far above simple logic and humanitarian concern for the earth and all its precious lifeforms.

So our advice would be this: fight the dump sites, stay as far away from a nuclear power plant as you can possibly get—move if you must, and write to your state representatives. Don't bother being radical, just remain within the guidelines of the law, but make your views known to someone who has the authority to initiate changes. Radical actions create disharmonic vibrations. You must always understand the people you're dealing with, the people you're attempting to change. Take a serious hard look at the Nuclear Regulatory Commission and try to logically reason out their "justified" thought process.

Do you really believe you'd get anywhere with the people who spent years and years of expensive and intensive research investigating the geological safety factors of a nuclear power plant site and *then* build the Diablo Canyon Plant near a major faultline in California? Where's the logic? The concern for life? Where is the high-tech intelligence of our advanced scientists? Write your representatives and just maybe, if enough respond, an unforeseen probability will be created by your joint efforts and the nuclear devastation will be averted. I'd like to believe that. I'd like to believe that people care enough to save the earth—to save their fellowmen.

And the Phoenix tensed its great talons into the soft earth while the people rioted in their discontent.

After several long debates between us and our knowledgeable friends, I came to the conclusion that this phase of the changes could be considered positive; not completely, but it did possess good aspects to it. Rioting is a terrible thing to witness, much less to be actively involved in. However, I'm an excessively peaceful person and I hold firmly that a riot is no justification of means no matter what good end it affects in the final outcome. To me, the end was the only good aspect. Yet, No-Eyes reassured me that very few people would actually be injured, as it was to be a *destructive* revolt—not a *killing* one. The end result was racial and religious equality for all.

However, this time period could not escape its ultimate phase. That of the nuclear exchange. Bill was successful in finding out how the exchange was to come about. I never did ask. Yet he offered one choice morsel of information for me to ponder over. He asked me if it ever crossed my mind that a fatal mistake would actually occur at one of the missile command centers of a country. Well, living here near NORAD, we hear about the incidents of near-mistakes that are made. It's not secret, it's in the newspapers. We also recently read a statement made by a former colonel who admitted that for every one that is publicized, ten more near-mistakes are not. But to think that an actual button would mistakenly be pushed by a country, a signal misread or a computer malfunction occur was unthinkable—until now.

And the Phoenix crouched while the world righted itself.

This was to be the grand civil unrest, the greatest peoples' revolt in all of history. Remember the altercations between nations? Now is the time people will refuse war. They will refuse to send their beloved sons off to undeclared fighting regions. The masses have endured enough repression and suffering. Their collective consciousness unites to bring about a better world. They can endure no more. They simply sit down to resist wars, taxes, and harmful political policies. And the awareness reaches up into the highest level of the government. Arguments ensue. A major exchange of high-ranking officials takes place and the policies are reversed. Peace reigns over the land and government is once again for and by the people. Unity prevails.

The shadow of the free-flying Phoenix crossed silently over the land and the world is one with the earth.

This was the ultimate end for the changes. This is why they began in the first place. Now, all races will be equal. All men will live and work and play as a total unit of humanity. The barriers will be torn down. But what will be most beautiful, will be the *way* in which man lives. No-Eyes showed me a most unique new civilization whereby technology developed innovative energy sources. The problem of gravity was conquered by a method which enabled man to reverse and control the magnetic polarity of the earth. This one discovery has endless ramifications.

All the lower lifeforms will be allowed to roam untouched. People will have learned to eat according to the Earthway. They will have devised new construction techniques and structures. They will cultivate high-yield protein crops and will have halted world hunger. They will join in a universal worship and recognize their planet as a living entity that freely supplies all their needs. They will be one in a brotherhood of humanity. They will be one with all of life as they recognize the peace of living the Way of the Indian nation—the Earthway.

The following listing represents the order of the Phoenix chronicles as No-Eyes foresaw them happening, however, we must bear in mind the law of probabilities that is constantly coming into play whenever future events are foreseen.

At the time of the lessons, she admitted to the strong possibility of several of the events occurring simultaneously. And now, we must be mindful that any of the happenings may, in fact, occur simultaneously or in other orders. What is important here is not the carved-in-stone order, but the *knowledge* of these things-to-come and our awareness to recognize the signs and our ability to make corresponding adaptations.

I am not a fortune-teller and have never claimed to be one. I merely conveyed the old visionary's words as she wished me to—as I had promised her I would. Nor am I a radical who incites discord within our magnificent country.

I firmly believe that the United States is the most beautiful country in which to live. I believe that our democratic form of government has the peoples' best interest in mind and that it can work for the people.

I live within the law and encourage everyone else to do the same. I encourage everyone to love one another, to listen to one another and to open your hearts to one another. Search deep within self to discover the brilliant truth that softly pulses there.

Phoenix Rising was not intended to depress the hearts and minds of mankind. If you read between the lines and under the surface of the concepts, you will clearly discover that mankind is forever strong and resilient, that it will ultimately overcome all obstacles to unite in a bond of peace to triumph as the victor in a universal brotherhood of man.

Perhaps that now we are aware of what is coming, man will uplift his mental attitudes, confront threatening forces, and make alterations and realizations as to his ultimate joint future. Perhaps the positive force of these corrective activities will indeed alter some of that which was to be. Perhaps man, through his new heightened awareness, may indeed circumvent some of the more devastating events. The advantage of viewing the future ramifications of present-day actions is, after all, a precious "gift of opportunity" to alter those negative avenues that would appear to bring forth harm and devastation.

We must cherish the advantage of clear foresight, value its knowledge, and utilize it to work toward achieving a unified future world—one of human compassion, deep spirituality and world peace.

The Phoenix Chronicles

Contractions/Economics Aspects
Massive blue collar strikes
Relocation of key factories overseas
Computerization of factories
Extended import/export embargos/taxations
Increased unemployment
Widespread factory shutdowns
Excessive taxation
Small business failures
Insolvency of many banks
Stock Market misdealings/decline
Drastic construction decline
Devaluation of real estate
Increase in corporate crime
Drop in level of manufactured goods
Increase of corporate monopolies/take-overs
Increase in personal bankruptcies
Widespread layoffs
Runaway credit purchases
Cash as only accepted tender

Emerging/Natural Disasters
Major devastation in California
Earthquakes in new areas
Inactive craters become unsettled
Mountains become unstable
Return of the dust bowl
Record breaking flooding
Tornados increase intensity and occasion
Liquefaction of soil beneath faults
Intensified hurricane devastation

Freak wind gusts/accidents
Soil erosion
Increased radon levels
Rock/mud slides
Insect infestation
Sink holes
Rapid temperature inversions
Frigid winters/deadly blizzards
Summer storms with intensified hail/lightning
Seeping natural gas (fires/explosions)
Underground fires
Widespread surface blazes
Major quake of the New Madrid Fault (southern Illinois or northeastern Arkansas) which may jeopardize the entire Mississippi River Valley area.
Greenish hue to atmosphere—Phoenix Days
Higher pollution levels

Eyes Searching/Transportation Accidents
Plane crashes increase
Shipping disasters increase
Higher incidents of train derailments/accidents

Listening/Freak Deaths & Accidents
Amusement park disasters
Increase in homicide/suicide
Freak household accidents
Disease outbreaks
Several catastrophic propane explosions
Germ Warfare release accident

Breath Heaving/Discord Between Nations
Grave economical differences
Arms escalation
Warring altercations
Terrorism increases
Undeclared wars
Clandestine dealing between countries
High level secrecy

Wings Flexing/Spiritual Unrest and Awakening
Questioning masses
Political church actions

Government interventions
Repression from certain religious sects
Increased U.F.O. sightings
Interaction with other intelligences
Acceptance of paranormal
Acceptance of ongoing spirit/afterlife
More religious sects going to court to force their personal restrictions on general public.

The Wailing/Nuclear Incidents
Several close meltdowns/leaks
Seeping radioactive dump sites
Two catastrophic meltdowns
Radioactive pollution of land/rivers
Several major accidents of nuclear missile truck carriers and the transportation of radioactive waste.
Radioactive releases caused from geological instability.

Talons Tensing/Civil Unrest
Peoples' revolt and resistance movements
Draft evasion
Public's discovery of coverups
Nuclear exchange

Crouching/Massive revolts and Government Turnaround
Taxation refusals
War resistance
Policy disagreements within government body
Major upheaval within governments

Flying Free/Rise of the Age of Peace
Total equality among people
Discontinuance of all meat ingestion
Construction reforms
Cessation of most severe natural disasters
Pollution-free energy innovations by way of the earth's magnetic field
Rise of the Indian Nation through widespread adaptation of its Ways of natural living and deep human philosophy.

Sign of the Times— A Personal Perspective

The following is directly related to the coming changes. It is most relevant because it involves what is happening today in the world of enlightenment teaching and its corresponding movement toward the attainment of spiritual awareness, human compassion, and world peace. I am compelled to speak out now, as this is the only opportunity I have to do so.

Following the release of the initial introductory book of the No-Eyes series, *Spirit Song,* I received beautiful readership mail from people all across the U.S. Clearly, No-Eyes' tender heart and profound wisdom had reached out to touch many hearts and awaken many spirits. I wish now to deeply thank you for all your wonderful encouragement for me to continue writing. I have every intention of doing so, for the telling of my warm experiences with the aged visionary and others like her, coupled with the ancient wisdom and universal philosophies they had to impart, will ultimately fill many more volumes—the next four books are ready and waiting. Your expressed high interest, your thirst for more, would've warmed the old one's heart.

Your intense response to *Spirit Song* has been overwhelming. In the many letters I've received, there is vivid evidence of a wonderful mass awareness dawning within the spirits of man. People are waking up out of their indifference and are listening to the nebulous urgings of their knowledgeable spirits. They now realize how vitally critical this present timeframe is, and they've come into the enlightening realization that they now need to shed the mundane facets of their lives in order to facilitate inner change—that of gathering their inner forces and going about accomplishing the superceding business of their spirit's path and purpose. They're telling me of deep, subtle promptings to relocate to other geographical regions—particularly the southwestern and mountain areas—where they know they have important spiritual goals to accomplish.

Many have expressed their private recognition of subtleties moving upon the land. They have personally perceived the initial stirrings of thousands of tattered and worn moccasins presently shuffling into position for the coming Great Unifying Event. And, although these cognizant individuals represent all races, their hearts and spirits retain ancient memories and, within this current timeframe, they have made this important sojourn to join forces for the prime purpose of nourishing the Sacred Tree and completing the Great Hoop of Man.

And, some readers write simply because they felt compelled to do so, often not even knowing why they're writing, or what they want to say—they simply needed to "touch." It is these letters that have been penned from the warm glow of the spirit. No-Eyes had reached out to touch their hearts and to spark their beautiful spirits into a renewed and heightened awareness. It has been an exquisite thing to see, and all these things are indeed wondrous. They serve to underscore my commitment to No-Eyes, and my heart rejoices that her tender life and high purpose has not fallen by the wayside, lying unnoticed, but has instead been lovingly embraced by so many truly beautiful people.

All of this positive readership correspondence gives valid credence to the hard and undeniable fact that the "seeking of expanded enlightenment" for our times is a high priority matter, and it remains a high demand subject of interest. It is this subject matter that I feel the urgent need to address now because it is such a grave concern of mine.

Various readership mail has served to widen my view of the many presently operating organizations, groups, centers, and individuals out there who are offering a myriad of enlightenment information that range in subject matter from natural health and nature meditation trips to environmental innovations and paranormal classes. Whether these centers be for corporeal or spiritual awareness is not necessarily relevant to my point. Whether the organizers possess the necessary background credentials and experience is irrelevant also. I realize that most of these peoples' intentions are usually good; however, it is the *manner* of their operation that greatly distresses me.

My readers have sent me all manner of pamphlets, newsletters, advertisements, and magazines produced by these various enlightenment organizations. Some of the material has been clearly homemade, while others have been the expensive glossy products of high technology. Still, I have no problem or reservations with either type of format.

What I adamantly object to is that most of these organizations, whether non-profit or not, have the bold audacity to claim enlightenment on the one hand while placing something as *un*spiritual as a common "pricetag" on what they have to offer the sincere seeker in the other hand. The two are diametrically in opposition. And this widespread practice appalls me. It speaks of *self*-serving intentions, of *personal* gain at the hands of innocent seekers of light.

The fact that there are teachers of spiritual truths and/or teachers of innovative environmental living who are actually "charging" exhorbitant admissions, fees and/or dues for seminars, symposiums, courses and the like is in direct opposition to the very basic *premise* of spirituality! To create a common "commodity" or "purchased product" out of enlightenment is to vulgarize the total *concept* of spirituality! True and pure spirituality has been taken out of the "sharing" of enlightenment to transform it into what is now disgustingly seen as the "selling" of enlightenment.

What this converts to is a stomach-turning statement that goes exactly like this: "Unless you come up with the money, you don't get spiritual enlightenment."

Do these outrageous pricetags mean that *only* those who can *afford* them are entitled to enlightenment, wisdom, information, or help? Is enlightenment then only for the *wealthy*? Is the majority of the population *barred* from such knowledge of light simply because the seekers cannot *afford* it? It certainly appears so and with the approach of such critical times when so many, many are reaching out for spiritual meaning, this situation is totally *unacceptable*!

In the beautiful tradition of the Indian Way, the concept of the Great Give-Away *should* be uppermost in the minds of today's teachers of new learning. The Great Give-Away is simply the humble giving, the sharing, of what we have to offer others. Whether this offering be spiritual wisdom, enlightened philosophy, life guidance, ecological environment innovations or just plain human comfort to one in need, makes no difference whatsoever. To give *freely* is the Indian Way. It is the way of human spirituality. To give *without* Expectation of recompense of any kind is the true Indian Way. It is the way of *true* human spirituality. To give just because that is the human spiritual thing to do is the Indian Way.

Look you to nature. All the magnificent gifts of nature are given free to man. It is natural to give. Enlightenment, no matter on what subject it is given, is only vulgarized by the clinking of coins into the palms of the giver. This horrendous practice *must* cease. It *must* be turned around if true spirituality is to flourish upon the land. The organizers and founders of these learning and informative centers *must* seek other means of gaining their monies than from the pockets of these sincere and innocent seekers. A great travesty is being perpetrated upon those who wish to gain some measure of expanded awareness. It must cease if man is to experience true and pure human

163

spirituality in a united bond of living together with the sweet earth.

Peace. Love. Giving. Spirituality. Humanness. Enlightenment.

These gentle words are simply mere shells without the *absence* of expectation on the part of the giver.

Empty rhetoric. Verbosity. Hypocrisy. Greed. False leaders.

At best, the "pricetag beings of enlightenment" are well meaning but sad, misguided individuals.

Please, this timeframe is far too critical for the earnest seeker to have to "pay" for that which he so desperately is seeking. It is too important to veer off your spirit's path only to end up listening to lectures, seminars, courses, or symposiums that require your money to maintain its very existence. Hear me, please. The blood of the seeker must *never* nourish the veins of the teacher! The teacher must be nourished from *within* rather than to drain that which is without! A true One of wisdom, a high teacher, *never* takes . . . but rather gives! Keep this tenet in mind—enlightenment is a universal entity of itself, therefore it is owned by no one, therefore no one can sell that which he owns not.

Because of the many letters we receive from my readers, we've established an enlightenment center called The Mountain Brother-hood. This is operated out of our home and was formed as a base whereby seekers can obtain answers to their many questions stem-ming from the various philosophical concepts and subject material No-Eyes taught. We are here to answer all correspondence on any of the wide variety of subjects covered by No-Eyes and written about in the series of books.

We've received inquiries, both general and specific, on subjects regarding health and natural healing, the future of man, the para-normal, Indian Ways, personal spiritual paths, lifestyles, the specific safety factors of particular geographic regions, etc. Always, we respond as quickly as possible. We also meet with those individuals who are, or who will be, in our area. We are committed to assist anyone who wishes such assistance, guidance, or sharing.

Those I've actually met with have been from all walks of life, incomes, and races. They've been farmers, ministers, professors, laborers, presidents of corporations, and even a Hopi elder. Young, old, rich or poor, makes no difference, for all are equal to me.

Some come in shyness, which soon dissipates. Some have come to say I must be a new leader, which is quickly denied. And some have come to boldly display their knowledge of psychic abilities, which are soon smothered by me (spiritual talents are *not* a sideshow)! Yet there have also been others who've come to "test" the author, which stems from their own inability to accurately perceive. This sort of encounter is either countered by me or it is completely ignored, depending upon the individual.

I do *not* meet with people to praise their attained talents, nor to defend and prove that which I know, nor to *be* praised. I meet with them just to sit over a cup of coffee and to listen to their words of concern or questions. They know they can speak freely with me. They know that I won't embarrass them (although I've been known to put the arrogant in their places a time or two). I meet with people simply to offer any help that I can that will enrich their lives or spirituality, or to add clearer definition to their pathway through life. I meet with them to listen to them talk because they know I'll understand.

So many people feel so alone. This is a time when all of us, as members of the family of man, must open our hearts and let our beautiful compassion flow to others. We are all drifting on the warm current of life and together we must be as lifeboats to those who feel they are sinking. We must not be fearful to hold out our hands and give companionship along the way. We must not be fearful to touch.

For me, there *are* not and truly *cannot* be "any ulterior motives of self-gain" in what I am doing. For indeed, that is not my way. That is not in keeping with the beautiful Tradition of the Great Give-Away that lives within my heart. That is not in keeping with the true light of human spirituality that pulses within my spirit.

Perhaps when this ugly subject of "paying" for enlightenment, simple guidance and/or help really hit home with me was when an elderly Hopi wiseman appeared unexpectedly upon my doorstep. At the time I wasn't home, but when he later called, what he asked me plunged my heart to the ground. He softly said, "How much do you charge for a consultation appointment?"

I was so taken aback by the shocking question, I was entirely speechless for a few seconds. "Why, nothing!" I said.

The man on the phone chuckled lightly under his breath. "Well, you know how much everything *costs* in the white man's world," he added.

I sighed. "Yes, I know, but I don't walk that path." My heart was sad at this realization. "This isn't the same trail," I answered, "this isn't the same one at all."

When I'd hung up, the full impact of his question struck hard. I considered what he had said about the "cost" of just talking and it literally sickened me. As knowledgeable as No-Eyes was, as profoundly wise and intensely powerful as her lessons were, she was the epitome of humility and compassion. How can others, who haven't a modicum of her wisdom and timeless vision, have the bold audacity to "charge" others for their personal guidance? It was a situation that went against everything No-Eyes had taught about everyone being loving members of the family of man. It went against everything she stood for. It went against the precious life and cherished memory of No-Eyes herself.

When it is feasible for us to do so, we are going to relocate into the central mountains of Colorado where we've been guided to a beautifully remote and virgin region where a clear river rushes year round through the property that borders a high mountain lake—where we'll finally be living within our long-awaited for sacred ground.

Until we are relocated, we welcome your correspondence sent to us in care of the publisher.

May Peace reside within your hearts and may Truth burn brightly within your beautiful Spirits.

Mary Summer Rain

" . . . . and when the great Phoenix is flying free, look closely at what he carries lovingly within his clenched talons. It will be a new green leaf, not from an olive branch, but from the new fresh growth of the Sacred Tree that will be flourishing straight and strong within the Hoop of Mankind's new Nation."

—No-Eyes